NEW HEAVENS

Series Editors
Walter J. Boyne and Peter B. Mersky

Aviation Classics are inspired nonfiction and fictional accounts that reveal the human drama of flight. The series covers every era of military and civil aviation, is international in scope, and encompasses flying in all of its diversity. Some of the books are well known best-sellers and others are superb but unheralded titles that deserve a wider audience.

NEW HEAVENS

My Life as a Fighter Pilot
and a Founder of the Israel Air Force

For behold, I create new heavens and a new earth;
And the former things shall not be remembered or come to mind
But be glad and rejoice forever in what I create;
For behold I create Jerusalem for rejoicing,
And her people for gladness.
—Isaiah 65:17–18

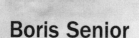

Boris Senior

Foreword by Peter B. Mersky
Foreword to the First Edition by Ezer Weizman

Potomac Books, Inc.
Washington, D.C.

Published in the United States by Potomac Books, Inc. (formerly Brassey's, Inc.). All rights reserved. No part of this book may be reproduced in any manner whatsoever without written permission from the publisher, except in the case of brief quotations embodied in critical articles and reviews.

Library of Congress Cataloging-in-Publication Data

Senior, Boris.
    [Shamayim òhadashim. English]
    New heavens : my life as a Fighter pilot and a founder of the Israel Air Force / Boris Senior ; foreword by Peter Mersky ; foreword to the first edition by Ezer Weizman.
        p.   cm.
    ISBN 1-57488-679-7 (hardcover : alk. paper)
1. Senior, Boris.   2. Israel òHel ha-aòvir—History.   3. Israel—History, Military.   4. Israel-Arab War, 1948–1949—Aerial operations.   I. Title.
UG635.I75S4613   2005
956.04'2—dc22   2003021721

Printed in Canada on acid-free paper that meets the American National Standards Institute Z39-48 Standard.

Potomac Books, Inc.
22841 Quicksilver Drive
Dulles, Virginia 20166

First Edition

10   9   8   7   6   5   4   3   2   1

Contents

Maps

Foreword

THE establishment of the State of Israel in May 1948 caught the world by surprise, especially when this event was so quickly followed by a particularly nasty war between the Israelis and their Arab neighbors. Confrontations between Jewish settlers and their sworn enemies, who had lived in the region since before biblical times, were an unfortunate part of life for the new arrivals seeking a homeland after the horrors of the Nazi concentration camps. The influx of these refugees swelled the ranks of the new nation and forced a do-or-die defense that has yet to be resolved after more than fifty-five years.

The Israel Army of 1948 was far removed from the well-equipped, highly trained force the world has come to know and respect. It relied on a vast collection of volunteers from all over the world, and an equally large, disparate assembly of equipment, much of which had long since been discarded by its original owners after World War II. Cadres of ex-patriots from Europe, America, Canada, and South Africa bolstered the meager ranks of the native-born Israeli defense forces against the Arab League, whose might, at least on paper, seemed poised to hurl the Israelis headlong into the Mediterranean. In similar fashion, an influx of weapons from behind the Iron Curtain and from forgotten airfields in South America and Europe arrived to help the hard-pressed Israelis. Everything from discarded rifles to biplanes eventually helped defend the tiny struggling country that became a symbol of resistance to the world and a beacon of hope to people without a home.

Although Boris Senior may not be well known outside Israel, he played an important, even vital, part in the formation of the Israel Air Force (IAF) and in the War of Independence in 1948. Those who do know of his efforts and dedication hold an abiding respect and appreciation for this transplanted South African who nearly died after being shot down on a mission in 1945 for the Royal Air Force. Leaving the RAF after World War II, he brought his family's history of service to the formation of the State of Israel.

He used his own money to buy supplies and aircraft and fly them to Israel. He flew combat sorties in such widely differing aircraft as the Spitfire and, of all things, a Beechcraft Bonanza, a general-aviation type, known for its unique butterfly tail assembly, which he had bought with his own money.

Yet, with all his experiences, Senior maintained a deep understanding of the overall situation that still bedevils the Middle East, and in particular Israel and its neighbors. As a senior citizen, his fondest wish was to see the resolution of the age-old problems that result in so many Israelis and Arabs dying in attacks and counterattacks, more than fifty years after he helped birth the IAF. (As this book entered production, word came of Boris Senior's death at age eighty in April 2004.)

This memoir describes an earlier period when Senior and many like him were dedicated to getting Israel on its feet among the nations of the world. During that turbulent time these men did whatever it took to get the job done. Senior is direct and forceful as he describes his attempts to circumvent European security while desperately trying to get precious aircraft to Israel. Although soft-spoken and always hopeful that things will improve, Boris Senior had no problem heading into dangerous situations if the end would help his newly adopted country retain her place in the family of nations.

With a title that refers to a biblical passage, this first-time English edition of Boris Senior's wartime autobiography sheds a new and very personal light on the struggle that began as the establishment of a new country and its concurrent fight to maintain that nationality, and yet today, still persists as one of the world's primary conflicts between people who are, in reality, brothers.

Peter B. Mersky
Editor

Foreword to the First Edition

ABOUT a year ago, Boris Senior told me he had decided to write a book for the fiftieth anniversary of the founding of the State of Israel and to tell the story of the foreign volunteers, the "Machalniks," who joined the air service of the state in the making. He stressed that his main aim in writing the book was to tell of the rise of the state and the miracle that happened to the Jewish people between the most terrible period of its history, the Holocaust, and the wonder of the founding of an independent country and its War of Liberation. I knew that as always he would fulfill his promise and complete his mission in time.

When Boris had appeared in the skies of Israel about six months before the declaration of independence, he was the right man at the right time. At that time, it was becoming evident to our national institutions that a confrontation between us and the Arab world was inevitable. The forces of the Haganah and its commanders had been organized into military formations, but they had been trained mainly as infantry fighters. The air sector, as a result of the restrictions

Ezer Weizman in the cockpit of a Spitfire in 1948.

imposed by the mandatory administration, was limited to a flying club, the aviation arm of the Palmach and the flying school of the Irgun. At the outbreak of hostilities, we had only a few light aircraft with some pilots who knew how to fly them, but without the necessary ability to take part in the great struggle we would face.

In November 1947, immediately following the United Nations's decision to partition the country into two states, one Jewish, one Arab, I received a cable that said "arriving on . . . signed Boris Senior."

Boris was born in South Africa to a Zionist Jewish family.

He was an excellent fighter pilot who had taken part in many important missions in Italy during the decisive stages of World War II. I met him in the Palestine Club in London in 1946. We had both just completed our service in the RAF, and within a few days, we became close friends. We were both mad about flying and were deeply attached to the Zionist cause. We had already decided that our place was to be in an Israel Air Force, which was to arise in the distant, uncertain future. Boris never forgot this, and at the time, he said he would come to Israel. He arrived, first of the fighter pilots to come as volunteers from abroad, the Malchalniks, who came to fight in the War of Independence.

Immediately after his arrival, Boris joined the group of the first pilots of the air service, and among other missions, he participated in the historic sorties of the four light planes that air dropped ammunition to the Etzion bloc. After having seen the shortage of aircraft and pilots, he went to South Africa to recruit volunteers and to buy aircraft. When they eventually reached Israel, they tripled our air strength.

In July 1948 some of our gifted technical staff succeeded in building a complete Spitfire from scrap and from parts of Egyptian aircraft we had shot down. Boris agreed to be the first test pilot to fly the improvised craft, though we were not sure it could take off and land in one piece.

Boris Senior, one of the first pilots of 101 Squadron, eventually found his place in the air force headquarters and was one of the pioneers who established guidelines for the organization and operations of the air force. But most of all, unlike most of the Machal pilots, he made his home in the country, raised a family, and became an Israeli citizen.

It remains for me to thank him for his contribution in general, and for having written of his part in the glorious history of the Israel Air Force.

Ezer Weizman
President of Israel
March 1998

CHAPTER ONE

A Yellow Stain in the Water

CERVIA, ITALY, MARCH 1945

THE target today is Mestre, the most heavily defended port in northern Italy. We are in 250 Squadron of the Royal Air Force flying Kittyhawk (P-40) fighters over northern Italy and in Yugoslavia, in support of the Eighth Army.

The readiness boards on the wall in the living room give out the day's duties. The hominess and familiarity of the living room are marred by the impersonal furnishings, such as the torn armchairs, and the carpets that are spread around the room, as well as by the general feeling of impermanence. We await the sign to man our aircraft, all the while pondering our fate.

Unlike the fighter interceptions, when we usually stand alert near the runway or in the cockpit ready for a "scrambled" takeoff, there is ample warning for bombing missions.

The runway is made of perforated steel planking, or PSP, sometimes known as Marston Mat, linked together in narrow strips to form a long, flat surface. Similar strips make up the taxiways. Nothing is permanent, for we have to be ready to dismantle everything and move forward if the ground forces are advancing, or back if we are retreating. The runway, too, can be easily taken apart and moved to another location. Airplanes are parked in their own parking bays among the trees and bushes. One mechanic services every two planes, helping us get into the machines and start the engines.

We get into the cramped cockpits of our Kittyhawks with our parachutes, life jackets, and dinghies, our maps strapped to our left thighs. The mechanic, kneeling on the wing, begins the start-up procedure. He turns the crank-handle faster and faster until the flywheel reaches a high-pitched whine. The magnetos are switched on, and the engine coughs and splutters into life. We check the various systems and increase to full power to test the engine. The Kittyhawk shudders and quivers, impatient at being restrained by the chocks.

We await the green Aldis-lamp signal from the control tower. As soon as the leader sees the green, he taxies out to the runway and opens up to full power. The takeoff is a hurried procedure, each fighter closely following the one in front to get aloft and into close formation. We have checked our radios but everything is done in radio silence for the time being. We are all well versed in our procedures and communicate using hand signals.

As the leader reaches 1,000 feet, he turns to port and we slide into a tight line-astern circle. When we are all in the circle the leader signals us into three flights of four airplanes in "finger" formation. Then, we set course to the north, well out to sea. I see the coastline below me and through the haze to the east, Yugoslavia.

Two Thirty-Nine Wing of the Desert Air Force, 250 Squadron's dive-bombers in the lead, is chosen to be first over Venice. Our wing probably has the most experienced fighter squadrons of the Desert Air Force. Its history is intertwined with the victories and the defeats from North Africa to southern Italy and now gives support to the Eighth Army by dive bombing and low-level strafing.

By this time, I had completed forty-five missions, some as fighter escort to the heavy bombers, but more frequently, performing interdiction flights to disrupt enemy transport lines by bombing bridges, railroads, and marshaling yards. The enemy has difficulty in moving anywhere behind his front lines during the day. Moving shipping and barges in the canals and rivers is also dangerous because of our constant presence.

RADIO SILENCE

In a long climb to attack altitude, grouped behind, below, and on both sides, wing upon wing of fighters join us. Sleek Mustangs, dainty Spitfire IXs, snub-nosed Thunderbolts with their huge radial engines, and the solid old Kittyhawks named after Kitty Hawk, the airfield of Wright Brother fame and almost identical to Gen. Claire Chennault's Flying Tiger fighters in China three years before.

Five hundred aircraft in a dive-bombing raid on one target, the largest assault of its kind in the entire European theater of operations. The target is beautiful, old Venice sinking slowly into its own mud, of interest now only for her ugly gray port of Mestre, a major supply center for the Wehrmacht forces in Italy. We know it bristles with anti-aircraft guns of every caliber.

During the briefing before takeoff, the details are given as usual by the intelligence officer, Flying Officer George. He is less jovial than usual—his pink English face and yellow eyebrows creased by an occasional frown. He says that we will approach from the sea to the east of Mestre harbor, dive on the ships in the harbor, and rendezvous out to sea at 5,000 feet after the bombing. With a view to avoiding damage to the city, only dive-bombers with their greater accuracy are employed. Because of the expected heavy anti-aircraft fire, Marauder [American-built B-26 medium bomber] "flak ships" will fly overhead to draw fire and, crucial as it turns out later for me, three air-sea rescue aircraft, one American and two British.

They are to follow and to wait over the sea south of the target area. One of the aircraft, an RAF Wellington, is fitted with a life boat, which can be dropped near any pilot who ditches in the sea. Another is a very old and slow Walrus single-engine seaplane of the Royal Air Force. The third is a twin-engine Catalina amphibian of the U.S. Army Air Force. [The army flew navy PBYs, designating them OA-10s.—ed.]

The sun glints through the haze and my eyes ache from the strain of searching the sky for enemy fighters. The Perspex of the windscreen and side panels is slightly scratched, yet my vision is largely unimpaired. The cockpit has the familiar smell of fuel, oil, and Glycol coolant. The faint smell of the harness webbing and parachute covers brings me back to the early days of my flight training and to my first solo in the Tiger Moth. I wriggle into a more comfortable position on the hard dinghy beneath me. My scalp itches and I try, though I know it to be useless, to scratch through the leather helmet.

The comforting drone of the engine is my sole companion on these long flights, and my only contact is the voices on the radio from the rest of the squadron. I search every sector of the gray sky behind me because that's where danger lurks, especially with the sun behind you. The enemy will attack from above and behind, invisible between you and the sun.

We constantly scan for possible attackers, maintaining radio silence until we are into our dive and are detected by the enemy. My mouth is parched, and I lick my lips so I can speak into the microphone in my oxygen mask.

I keep my goggles on all the time to protect my eyes from the flames that may engulf me in a crash landing or from a strike by enemy aircraft or anti-aircraft fire. Hundreds of gallons in the fuel tank are two feet in front of me. For the same reason, I fly with long leather gloves. Some of my comrades have suffered badly burned faces from their exploding aircraft, but some continue to fly missions in spite of it.

To the left I can see Lake Comacchio just inland from the coast beyond Ravenna and the rivers that flow out at right angles from the coast. The small towns along the coast are harmless and barely worth a glance, for the heavy anti-aircraft batteries are farther inland near the cities of Ferrara and Bologna. Smog and haze merge the sky and the sea into an indistinct blur as I peer through my windscreen at the murky horizon. The sea lies in wait far below, sluggish, lifeless, reflecting the yellow-gray haze above it.

I muse about the force of air-sea rescue aircraft assigned to the operation, and I double-check my yellow Mae West life jacket. High above us are the two South African Spitfire squadrons, weaving protectively.

The aircraft of my flight form around us with practiced skill. Blue and Green flights of my squadron, in the middle distance are on the left and right of my Red flight, one slightly below and the other above. All seem suspended motionless in the haze. The hundreds of aircraft in the other wings are just barely discernible in the far distance behind our wing, which is leading the attack. Dive bombers, each carrying two 500-pound bombs or one 1,000-pound bomb, drone northward over the Adriatic toward our target.

From time to time the Spitfire escorts criss-cross gracefully above us as they search the sky for enemy fighters. It is insulting for us as fighter squadrons to be protected by other fighters while we are now temporarily relegated to a mission of precision dive-bombing, but our heavy bomb loads will make us vulnerable to interception and unwieldy in the dogfights that must follow.

FINGER OVER THE SEA

To the east across the sea is Yugoslavia, which we have attacked less often in these last few months of the war, for our maximum effort is concentrated now on Field Marshal Kesselring's forces as they retreat to the north of Italy.

To the west, the setting sun helps us to pinpoint the twelve aircraft of the nearest squadron, which is divided like all the others into three flights of four craft like ours. Each flight is at a different altitude, separate yet together, each pilot watching the tail of the aircraft nearest to him, each flight watching the other two flights of its squadron, each squadron guarding the one next to it. At every turn the outside aircraft dives under its partner toward the inside of the turn to take up its position on the opposite flank, each flight in turn performing the same diving turn under its neighboring flight. A gigantic ballet in the sky, reaching into the distant haze.

This finger formation was introduced during the Battle of Britain and is dictated by the iron rule of self-preservation. Separated most of the time by the immensity of the sky, at other times there are moments of dangerous proximity during the long sliding turns. Your neighboring aircraft wheels under or over you, showing its graceful cockpit canopy or its underside streaked black by fumes. It's a momentary surprise as you recognize the head hunched under its leather helmet with the oxygen mask concealing the features, and then arcing off into the distance and to anonymity again. You disregard the earth below until you begin your landing approach or until you are in trouble. And the sea, set in its freezing snow-covered shores, dominates the environment below us, waiting.

The comradely formation of the squadron breaks up in a split second when contact is made with enemy fighters, and a wild individual scramble starts. All the rules of good flying are cast aside as you maneuver for position, G-forces clutching at the flesh on your face and turning your limbs to lead while your vision dims.

The 1,400-horsepower Allison engine hums reassuringly in front of me. I check the oxygen flow, adjust the face mask closer to the contours of my cheekbones and jaw, and feel the cold seeping into my feet despite my thick fur-lined suede flying boots. Some pilots refuse to wear them, knowing that in case of a bailout, the violent jerk when the parachute opens will make them drop off, leaving you to try to get back to your lines shoeless. A trace of black smoke from the exhaust of one of the aircraft reminds me to adjust my mixture control as we gain altitude.

How attached one becomes to the aircraft one flies in combat. After having flown the Hurricane, Spitfire, and Mustang, I became a sworn advocate of the Kittyhawk, not only for its great flying characteristics but for its ability to take unbelievable punishment and yet make it back to base. Last week, the Canadian, Jim Duval, the only married pilot in the squadron, made it back to base in his Kitty with one-third of its starboard wing-panel covers gone.

I check the oxygen supply line and fiddle with my radio's squelch button to ensure I will hear as clearly as possible in the din that will begin after radio silence is broken over the target. We have passed the front line now and are deep into enemy territory. On the left I see that we are past Lake Comacchio, and far ahead of my port wing the snow-covered coastline leads to Venice in the distance. As the coastline begins to turn east in a big loop toward Trieste, I see Venice with its anti-aircraft batteries.

I recall yesterday's mission in which we roamed at low level, searching for moving transport. We strafed and destroyed vehicles on the roads and barges in the canals and rivers. I recall a woman running in panic to her farmhouse as we suddenly appeared over the fields with a deafening roar. I got a glimpse of her white petticoat as she ran, and I quickly stopped firing my six guns.

MESTRE

The coast is partly veiled by low clouds and haze and runs parallel to our course. Now we fly deeper into enemy territory, weaving as we guard against getting jumped by German fighters from their bases in southern Austria. I glance at the coastline to the left in an effort to read our exact position relative to the target. When we are sure of our location abeam Venice, we level out at 9,000 feet and turn toward land to get into position for the bombing dive. I make a final check of fuel mixture, propeller pitch, and fuel tanks before pulling the lever to arm the bombs. As I await the carpet of anti-aircraft shells through which we have to dive, the tension increases. More than seventy guns protect our target in Mestre, not counting those around Venice itself.

The wing commander gives a signal with his raised fist and we move rapidly into echelon formation preparing to dive. Another few seconds and the ack-ack will begin to explode around us. I see the rest of my squadron advancing with me toward the target, the aircraft bobbing up and down in the turbulence, and I feel close to them. I am comforted by their presence, though there is nothing much we can do for each other if things go wrong.

Now that the enemy knows we are here, we break radio silence, and I mark the tension in our voices. As we get nearer the target, the anti-aircraft shells begin to explode around us, white for the Bofors at about 6,000 feet. They appear to be harmless but are the most dangerous. The oily black patches from the 88mm guns burst much higher and so are less dangerous for us.

I keep my leader in view and stay as close as possible without crowding him. I know that this is the big one, the best-defended city in northern Italy. This raid on Venice is the climax of our campaign, and its defenses make it a dangerous and difficult task.

Before entering the dive, I give a last quick glance upward and note the Marauder flak ships flying through the bursts of fire from the 88mm guns. They continue on their course as though they are oblivious of the firing and I realize that there is not much they can do about it because they are much slower and less maneuverable than our Kittyhawks.

We make a sharp, wheeling turn to the left, and the squadron moves into echelon formation behind us. Without warning, we run into anti-aircraft fire; I weave wildly, changing direction and height every two or three seconds to dodge the gunners and their predictors. It's my good luck to be number two to the wing commander and to dive right behind him. It will take the ack-ack crews a few more minutes to get their sights set, and by then I'll be into my dive and climbing away.

With radio silence gone, my earphones snarl with orders and staccato phrases interspersed with the static. The bursting of the anti-aircraft shells all around us and the deafening shouts on the radio from the rest of my wing confuse me as I get ready to enter the dive. The flak now looks thick, but my fears recede as I remember that I have already flown forty-five missions and made it back to base every time. As the flak gets thicker, we weave violently as we try to confuse the German gunners below. Hell, I've never seen stuff like this before. And we have to dive through it all.

Through the haze and smoke of the flak bursts, I make out a large ship berthed at the dock with what looks like a big torpedo boat and a tanker on the outside of the pier with massive sheds and warehouses. We are to concentrate on the big vessel, the *Otto Leonhardt,* and to leave the tanker and the shore installations for the following squadrons of dive-bombers. Hopefully one of us will hit the large ammunition dump in the port area and cause great damage. I can make out some of the gun emplacements spread out around the target area and the flashes from their guns.

I see another quick signal with his fist from the wing commander on my left as he pulls up and rolls over onto his back and down into the long dive. I select full-rich mixture for the lower altitude, and with a quick glance at the red gun sight, I follow him down in a near-vertical dive of 8,000 feet.

I see him in his diving left turn right under me, and I see a big, black ship far below as I roll my Kitty into the long dive, stamping on the left rudder pedal as the increased air speed causes the craft to slew to the right. Despite the strong pull to the right with the speed increasing furiously, I keep the black ball of the turn-and-bank indicator in the center. This is proof that I am not skidding to one side and ensures that my bomb will fall along the correct trajectory to the target. The Kitty shudders and shakes from the buffeting air, and the scream of the slipstream becomes so loud that I pay little attention to the flak bursting around me. Suddenly, there is an explosion nearby and my fighter lurches to the left. Another and another, and then a sickening thump as I feel a hit near the tail.

Too late now, I'll carry on the dive. I see the ship racing toward me, squat and ugly next to the pier and sheds. I keep the gun sight steady and slightly below the ship as I close in upon it. I pull back on the stick and edge the sight up through the center of the vessel, hold for perhaps half a second, and then press the bomb-release button. I feel a familiar lightening of the aircraft, and I pull back on the elevator with all my strength as she seems determined to stay in the vertical dive. Now I realize that my craft is badly hit, perhaps mortally. Knowing that the elevator controls have been hit, I pull back farther, one foot braced against the dashboard to gain increased leverage.

I am relieved as the nose comes up, though slowly and reluctantly. For an instant, I see masts ahead and I am shocked to see that they are above my eye level. I feel a tremendous, heaving lift as the bomb hits the ship, but far too close to my aircraft. My Kitty shudders from the blast of the explosives, and pieces of the bomb burst strike the belly and underside of the wings as I pass directly over the ship. Relieved to find I still have control, I begin to skid my machine wildly as I zoom up and away from the flak. As I turn out to sea, the Kitty mushes upward but too damn slowly, emitting a stream of white glycol coolant liquid.

HEADLONG FALL

I doubt I can make it back to base. I am too far from our lines, and if I bail out, it will be over the freezing sea. If I head back to land, I will become a prisoner of war. I can reach the German-held coast, but I decide to head out to sea in the hope of ditching safely in the water and getting picked up by our air-sea rescue forces. I give little thought to the consequences, my only worry now is how to cope with the immediate task of getting out of the aircraft in one piece. I find myself leaning forward and straining against my shoulder straps as though to urge the Kitty to greater height and distance. I scan my instrument panel, and as the airspeed drops rapidly, I ease the nose gently forward from its near-vertical attitude to a more-steady climb.

Breathing great gulps of oxygen from my mask, I try to gain altitude. The cylinder-head temperature gauge creeps into the red, and I know that I have only minutes before I have to abandon the aircraft.

Keeping my voice as calm as possible, I tell the wing commander in the aircraft ahead of me that I have been badly hit and am heading out to sea where I expect to bail out. I am comforted when I see the other three aircraft of my flight peeling off overhead and approaching to take up positions on either side of me.

The flak fades as I head out to sea, with only an occasional burst of 88mm above me. My engine runs roughly but the engine revs keep above 2,300. I watch the instrument panel as we climb through 5,000 feet. The cylinder-head temperature is at the end of the scale and decision time is near. I take a quick look down at the land behind me. The shore to the north and south of my position is covered in a white mantle of snow, portending an ice-cold ducking when I bail out. I have little time to weigh these two undesirable alternatives and hastily opt for bailing out over the sea in the hope of getting back to our lines if I survive in my dinghy.

Smoke pours into the cockpit. The engine runs rougher as the coolant streams out. Aiming for least resistance to the airflow, I pull the throttle back and move into full-course pitch to feather the propeller. My eyes behind the goggles smart and stream, and now I see a flicker of flame on the side of the firewall. Any minute now the fuel tanks may explode. The altimeter needle shows that the rapid climb has brought me up to higher than 5,000 feet. I am thankful my Kittyhawk can take this punishment. I see the cylinder-head temperature rising, and the engine runs rougher, thumping loudly.

I call the wing commander and try to sound cool as I say, "Topper Red Two heading for the rendezvous point, but I have to bail out. Please watch me." As I say this, the engine seizes up and I see the fire to the front and left of the windscreen. I keep the nose pointing to the southeast toward our front lines in the distance, all the while losing height. I know now that I cannot make it to our front lines. The smoke from the dead engine obstructs my vision. I continue to breathe oxygen through my mask but have difficulty seeing my instruments. I cough and wheeze as fumes penetrate my mask. I breathe smoke mixed with burning oil vapors. When I realize there is no hope, I unlock the canopy hood and roll it back. I take off my helmet and from force of habit drape it over the stick. I take a last look at the hostile coastline to the east and see the burning warehouses of Mestre as I unlock the harness. I see the dashboard with its instruments and my oxygen mask hanging uselessly from my helmet. Outside my cockpit the wings with the camouflage paint and the RAF roundels fill the view of my trusted kite. The Kittyhawk shudders violently as she enters the final phase of her death throes, and I try to abandon the aircraft. A moment of panic comes when I find I cannot move, until I realize that I have forgotten to release the shoulder straps. A quick tug on the release pin, and as I put my aircraft into a slow diving turn to the left, I glance at the sea far below, looking calm and peaceful, almost inviting.

I leave all systems operating and hesitate for a few agonizing seconds before I abandon the Kitty. I grip the cockpit side and clamber over the left wall of the cockpit. Now, the sea looks dark and threatening as I dive head first into the gaping void 5,000 feet below and think, *Just let me miss the tail and I'll have a chance if the chute opens.* I feel a searing pain in my foot as it glances off the tail. My life now depends upon a piece of equipment I had been sitting on for many hours of flying, something I had slung casually over my shoulder and dropped on the floor like a sack of potatoes. I had treated it with no more respect than a pair of old boots. I wish in those few moments of free fall that I had taken better care of my parachute. I wait a few more seconds with my hand on the cold metal parachute handle, delaying pulling the handle to ensure that the chute will not get entangled in the tail of the plane. Then a quick jerk on the handle and the chute opens above me, wrenching my body around but stopping my headlong fall.

After the frenzied tumult I have left, it is calm and an uncanny silence. I feel as though I am suspended in that huge sky, only the cool breeze blowing over my cheeks and upward through my hair, freed now of the leather helmet, which makes me realize that I am falling. The silence is broken by the deep thump of bombs and the sharper cracks of ack-ack over Mestre a few miles to the west. But at the same time, I have a feeling of utter loneliness as I look for my stricken aircraft. A minute later, I see the Kittyhawk plunge into the sea in one final dive, and as the sea closes around her, I feel I have lost something dear and close.

The big, incredibly beautiful canopy of the chute bulges above me as I sway gently below it. Over to one side below me but dangerously close, the docks of Venice exude clouds of smoke and dust with the sky above it peppered by anti-aircraft fire. I am close enough to make out the campanile of St. Marks and the Lido. In spite of dread at the fate in store for me, I am glad we have succeeded in our mission to destroy the main Axis port in Italy.

ALONE WITH MAE WEST

My thoughts quickly return to my own predicament and I prepare to hit the icy Adriatic. I look at the sea far below.

With momentum gathering deceptively slowly, it seems to loom toward me, and I realize that I shall soon plunge into it. I turn the parachute harness button and hold my fist in front of it ready to hit it smartly for releasing, knowing how many pilots have made a safe landing in the water, only to choke and drown in the harness and shrouds. I inflate my Mae West life jacket with a twist of the lever from under the flap and note with relief the shiny yellow material swell as the gas fills the life vest. I decide to wait a little and continue to fall. God, it's a good thing I didn't release. I must still have been a thousand feet up. Then a sudden shock as I hit the freezing water. All at once I hear a ghastly sound of retching and groaning.

I look around in astonishment for the source of the inhuman racket, only to realize that the source is me as I spew water from my lungs, all the while pushing and dragging the parachute away from my head. When I finally get free of it—just moments ago my salvation but now a threat to my life—I search blindly in the water under my buttocks until I find the dinghy package whose hardness I cursed on every flight. By the time I find the inflation bottle, my fingers are numb. I remember Rusty who had bailed out six weeks ago into the same sea east of Lake Comacchio only to be found frozen dead inside his dinghy two hours later.

I grope in the water below me, trying to remove the safety pin so I can unscrew the bottle to inflate the dinghy. But my frozen fingers cannot even feel the pin. After one last desperate effort, I realize it's a losing battle. The more I try, the more frozen my fingers become. When I realize the heavy dinghy package is dragging me down into the depths below I give up, unhook the dingy package, and watch it sink into the watery abyss beneath me.

As we started our dive on the ships, the radio silence ended and the racket in my earphones was overpowering. Now with my helmet and earphones gone, the wind blows gently through my hair and the peace and quiet around me seem unreal. The anti-aircraft guns booming from the nearby shore and the whine of the Merlin and Allison engines above form an uncanny background. I am completely alone immersed in what looks an endless cold ocean, with no contact to anyone who can rescue me. I see the yellow fluorescent dye from my Mae West staining the water around me. I pray my pal Tony above is keeping his eyes on my bobbing head in the slowly expanding patch of discolored water from my Mae West.

The three remaining Kittyhawks of my flight circle high above me as they try to keep me in sight among the waves. It is comforting to feel that I have not been abandoned, but I know that my chances of coming out alive are minimal. Apart from the paralyzing cold, which gets worse with every minute that passes, there is the virtual impossibility of being pulled out of the sea while under fire from the nearby German shore batteries.

As if someone has read my thoughts, I see vessels making for me at high speed, their wake churning the water into white foam. It must be the German E-boats we know are in the bay. My mind is in turmoil. Am I being left by our side to die in the cold or to become a prisoner of war?

I know my comrades' fuel is running low for they turn southward and become smaller and smaller, tiny specks in the sky. Now I know that I am abandoned, and in utter desperation I prepare myself for the end in the freezing sea or in a Nazi prison camp. Moments later, I am relieved to make out six Spitfires taking over and circling high above me, affirming that I have not been left to die on my own.

When I hear the firing of machine guns above me, I realize there is no way that Jerry will be able to come out and capture me, for the circling Spitfires are diving down low toward the E-boats near the shore, firing their machine guns and cannons. When the Spits get to the bottom of their dives just above me, I realize how close the Germans are from the deafening staccato of the exploding shells from the strafing.

In no time, the boats turn and retreat at high speed to the coast, zig-zagging as they try to escape the firing Spitfires. Though the attacking Spits have dashed my hopes of being pulled out by Jerry, I am hopeful now that my side may have some plan to get me out of this predicament before I succumb. Surely the attack of the Spits on the E-boats indicates that there may be some such attempt in the offing.

The time passes. My body is slowly becoming paralyzed from the cold, and I lose hope. I can see buildings and the campanile of St. Marks and estimate I am less than 800 meters from German-occupied Venice, right under the guns of those I have just bombed.

The numbness spreads to my legs and loins and to my arms. I see my mother in a summer dress in the garden in far-off South Africa. Memories come and go, and strangely while my body is freezing, I imagine I am back in the safe cocoon of my home and environment, in the familiar surroundings of my youth with my family beside me. Then when I realize where I am and what is ahead of me in this icy sea, I groan. I am lost, helpless, unable to do anything to free myself from the agony of this process leading to my death. There is no way out, for I cannot move my arms or legs enough even to try to propel my body to the land that is so close.

Gradually, I become still and I know I am freezing to death. My past races through my mind, some parts in clear outline, others in murky silhouette as life begins to drift away. My home, my life fades slowly away and becomes a hazy dream world.

CATALINA

By now I have been in the water for two hours, my sodden flying kit weighing me down. Yet, my life jacket keeps me afloat with my head just above water. I contemplate the irony of this slow, painful death next to the peacetime playground of the rich. I can still make out the campanile of St. Marco behind the Lido.

Apart from the noise of the bombing and the anti-aircraft guns, there is no sign of life. I am alone. My flying jacket and uniform are stained by the dye from the life jacket. I know I am getting weaker. My whole body starts to shake and shiver and my teeth chatter uncontrollably.

Suddenly, I see and hear high in the sky a large white aircraft approaching. I do not know whether it is coming for me. I don't even know how many Allied aircraft have been shot down and may have crashed into the water. I watch as the big white bird circles slowly and lands on the water. I see the wake of the big plane and the foam from its hull as it taxies toward me. Until it comes near, I am not sure that it is for me. As they come closer, I know that they have come for me. A sob escapes me.

But now, all hell breaks loose. The air fills with the shriek and whistle of salvo after salvo as the enemy gunners zero in on the flying boat, a sitting duck for the Germans on the nearby Lido. The Catalina throws a big wake as it bears down on me at high speed. As it nears a hatch opens halfway along the fuselage, and they throw me a rope. I grab for it, but it slips through my frozen fingers and I swallow seawater and retch as I am engulfed by the PBY's wash.

Under intense fire the crew keeps the aircraft moving at high speed. Time and time again, the flying boat circles and approaches me, the captain keeping it constantly on the move. The maneuver fails repeatedly as my frozen hands fail to grip the thick rope and my head goes under time after time.

After about fifteen minutes, I see a crewman in his bright yellow life jacket clamber out, run to the end of the big wing, and jump into the sea near me. The cold quickly overpowers the brave American, and the flying boat circles again and comes alongside him while his crew pull him back with difficulty into the flying boat. Now I fear that they are about to abandon the rescue and leave me to the mercy of the Germans or the icy water. But the captain perseveres, and the big white flying boat repeatedly taxies fast toward me on a circular path and the scene is reenacted. The firing from the shore batteries does not stop for a moment. It looks like the German gunners are getting their range for the shells get closer and closer.

After more vain attempts with the rope, I manage to keep hold of a long wooden boat hook they thrust at me. That is enough, and a moment later they lift me into the Catalina. I am no sooner in the aircraft when I feel the power surge of engines and we are quickly airborne and heading out of range of the German guns. Through the side of the bouncing aircraft, I hear the sound of the exploding shells near us.

The crew cut off my uniform, taking my wings, ranks, and insignia as souvenirs. By this time I am barely conscious and the puzzled Americans, not having seen a khaki South African Air Force uniform with red tabs on the shoulders, ask me what force I belong to, who I am, and I remember answering, "I am a South African Jew." The crew massages my frozen legs and arms, and I begin to feel the blood circulating in my limbs. I slowly return to full consciousness, but I am still in shock. As I lie on the rough blankets, all that is in my mind is relief at still being alive.

The Catalina gains height slowly as she heads out to sea along the Adriatic coast. In less than an hour, we reach the squadron runway where I had taken off a few hours before. The landing is difficult for the big craft on our narrow PSP strip in the sand dunes.

I am carried to my bed with my teeth still clattering. The peace and quietness of the little villa in Cervia seems to be another world, though only a scant twenty-five minutes flying time from the sea under the raging hell over Venice. The squadron pilots crowd around my bed with congratulations and a hundred questions. I am ashamed of my trembling jaws, which I fear will be seen as shivers of fright, but try as I might, I am unable to stop them from rattling loudly. The squadron doctor comes into my room, and after checking me, he says I will be fit for flying duties once I have properly thawed out.

The following morning I look at what is left of my uniform and my underwear from the day before, stained yellow with the dye that seeped from my Mae West life jacket. The Allied Military Government (AMGOT) money is stained yellow too, and I keep it as a memento of the raid on Venice. I visit the squadron parachute packers to thank them for providing me with the chute that saved my life. After that, I am bundled into a Kittyhawk for a test flight to ensure that my nerves are not shot. Soon I am back on active flying duty and more dive-bombing raids.

The American pilot of the Catalina received a well-deserved Distinguished Flying Cross. I would have liked to hear that the brave crewman who leaped into the water under fire to help me also received a medal. Years later in Israel, the U.S. air attaché tried to get details of the crewman's whereabouts without success, so all I have is his name "Al Feliksa," told to me while I was barely conscious in the PBY. [The pilot was 1st Lt. Jackson S. Dunn, and Sgt. Al Feliksa did receive the Silver Star and the Purple Heart for his attempt to rescue the author. Sergeant Feliksa had sustained injuries when he was apparently hit by fire from shore, although he didn't know it until he was back in the Catalina.—ed.]

Recently, I discovered that a friend of mine called Les was one of the pilots of a South African squadron during the

Venice raid and flew one of the six Spits detailed to escort the PBY on its rescue mission. By an extraordinary coincidence, he became a Mahal (volunteer) pilot in 101 Squadron in the Israel Air Force in 1948, and we flew missions together in Israel. I have talked to him about the raid. After realizing that it was me he saw in the drink, he told me of his grandstand view of the whole rescue operation. He said the captain of the PBY had radioed them saying that the pilot in the water was in a bad way. Les also described the attack on the German E-boats in the harbor of Venice, foiling their attempt to capture me.

After my return to active operations, the squadron was detailed to fly missions in Yugoslavia. Briefing sessions before takeoff emphasize that in case of a forced landing or being shot down over enemy territory, we were to try to be taken to Tito's forces and not under any circumstances to be captured by the Ustachis, Croat forces that cooperated with the Germans. Their nickname in the squadron was "ball hackers," because they had a habit of castrating pilots who fell into their hands.

After the Venice raid, our activities were concentrated mainly in the Yugoslav sector of operations. The raids across the Adriatic meant quite a long crossing over the same water in which I had nearly drowned. It was an effort to pluck up enough courage to make the flights, and it has taken me many years to cope with the fear of flying over the sea. However, I overcame it when I crossed the North Atlantic thirty years later solo in my own small Twin Comanche, passing over the freezing waters of the North Atlantic from Labrador to Greenland and Iceland before reaching England.

After a number of missions, I got a week's leave and hitched a flight to Cannes on the French Riviera. The city was full of troops on short leave from various battlefronts; most of them were American, the British contingent being limited to one small hotel, the Montana, where we were billeted. The seafront cafés with dark blue awnings looked so very Mediterranean and peaceful that it was difficult to remember we were only on a short respite before returning to combat flying.

MY BIG BROTHER LEON

The day after my return to the squadron someone said to me, "Sorry to hear about your brother." Shocked, I learned he had gone missing a week before I was shot down while flying his B-24 Liberator back from a raid on the marshalling yards of Udine in northern Italy. We had had no contact, apart from a very occasional postcard. He was stationed far back in southern Italy at Foggia in a South African Air Force wing while my RAF fighter squadron was near the front line.

A poignant letter from him was waiting for me, telling me that he had got hold of a Primus stove for me. Primus stoves were sought by all of us and were virtually unobtainable. My efforts to find out more details of what had happened to Leon were in vain, and after a few days I was ordered to return immediately to South Africa. When my sister Selma had entered my mother's bedroom in the morning to break the news, she gave one look and asked,

"Which one?" She behaved with the dignity that was part of her makeup. In despair and sorrow over Leon's death, my parents arranged for me to return home. They did not know at the time that they had nearly received two telegrams in one week announcing the loss of both their sons.

Leon never returned, and the only clue we have ever had about him was that the body of his bombardier was found in the sea just north of Venice, near where I landed in the sea. After completing his bombing raid, Leon had sent a coded radio message that he had accomplished his mission but nothing more was heard from him. I have subsequently seen a report that he was coned by searchlights and went down in flames after being hit by heavy anti-aircraft fire over the target.

Leon was six years older than me, and as my older brother was my role model. He was of medium height, a handsome young man, refined like his mother and somewhat reserved. With his big blue eyes and shy smile, women were immediately drawn to him, but being fastidious in his choice of everything, he was never involved in a string of shallow romances. Like other members of our family, he was an individualist. I remember him in high school, and he never ran with the herd socially. He was quiet and courteous with everyone, and I never heard him raise his voice. He could easily have completed his military service as a flight instructor in South Africa far from the perils of the air war in Europe but insisted on joining an operational bomber squadron in Italy. One of my two sons bears his name, which has been in my father's family for many generations.

My family and Leon's young wife, though still not giving

up hope, seemed to have come to terms with the news of Leon's missing in action. I witnessed only one heart-rending scene. When I passed Leon's room, I saw through the open door that Leon's wife was collecting his clothes to put away. I watched her for a moment and saw her clasp his uniform jacket and hug it closely to her. That small act in the silent bedroom has been with me ever since.

When I returned to Johannesburg after the Venice raid, I waited in South Africa for news of Leon, for I had agreed to my parents' wish not to return to operational flying until we heard about him. It was a difficult time for all of us. Until we heard that the body of one of his crew was found in the sea near Venice, we had kept hopes of his being a prisoner of war. As time passed we lost hope. In the meantime, the war ended in Europe. Understanding that I had to assume a more responsible role in the family, I sought my release from active service as soon as possible.

All that remains for us of my brother Leon, apart from our memories, is his name on a memorial column in Malta, which has the names of all the missing airmen of the Allied forces in the Mediterranean theater of war. Later, Dad financed the building of a community hall in the village of Kfar Shmaryahu in Israel on a hill that was renamed "Ramat Leon." He also established a permanent scholarship in Leon's name for South Africans at the Hebrew University of Jerusalem.

CHAPTER TWO

Heritage

LITHUANIA

MY father was born in Naumiestis, Lithuania, a pleasant village that serves as the hub of a prosperous farming region. Like most of Lithuania, it is in an area of green fields and broad rivers. The 1,600 Jews of the village made up half of the population and had their own synagogue, library, and school. They also set up a medical clinic and a small bank to grant loans to members of their community who needed financial assistance.

The Russians had occupied Naumiestis in the late 1700s. They instituted draconian laws of military service requiring quotas of recruits, some only twelve years old, from the villages for conscription into the Russian army for as long as twenty-five years. Many grandparents preferred emigration for their children even to such distant places as South Africa. For a long time, I couldn't understand my grandparents sending their progeny so far away knowing that they would probably never see them again. When I became aware of the alternative of serving in the Tsar's army for a third of their lifetime, I began to understand how they managed to cope with the separation.

It was in 1893, at the age of thirteen, that my father made his way to South Africa from his birthplace in Naumiestis. He went alone, probably by steamer across the Baltic to England and from there to Cape Town. How he managed it has always baffled me for I cannot imagine the months of travel and the difficulties he must have encountered on his lonely journey and arrival in the strange and distant country in Africa at the end of the nineteenth century. I have always regretted that I did not question him enough about his past, knowing only that when he arrived he worked in a small store in the veld, slept in a packing case, and boasted that he used to make himself a breakfast of ten eggs. He spoke no English.

At the close of the fourteenth century, continental European Jews who were fleeing persecution from the Crusaders came to Lithuania on the invitation of Grand Duke Vytautas (Witold), who ruled from 1392 to 1430. It was a haven of safety for them, and they were in some cases even granted privileges of the nobility. For a long time, I couldn't comprehend why the Lithuanians after so many years of fair treatment of their Jews suddenly started to kill them when the Germans conquered the country in 1941. They did not stop until they had murdered more than 95 percent of the entire Lithuanian Jewish population. One-quarter of a million men, women, and children, in some 300 villages and towns, were killed mainly by Lithuanians, who carried out the butchery for the Germans. Apart from the units of the

Lithuanian armed forces who did the mass killings, tens of thousands of Jewish citizens were murdered by the Lithuanians who had sat on school benches next to them.

In recent years when I began a quest to find my roots, I searched for a map of Lithuania. Someone brought me a large map more than a meter and a half in length. When I spread it out, I was astonished to see that of the 300 villages in which the Jews lived, the map was of my Dad's village. It was drawn by hand from memory by one of the few survivors of Naumiestis, a man who had immigrated to Chicago. Below the detailed drawing of Naumiestis that showed most of the owners' names and the location of the village houses on the eve of the Holocaust was a detailed report of the events of 1–2 July 1941, the dates all the Jews of Naumiestis were killed. The map, which I took with me on the visit to the village, also describes how in July 1941 all the Jewish women and children of the village were taken to the nearby forest in horse-drawn wagons after being told that they were on a journey to their husbands who were "working in Germany." They were killed in front of hurriedly dug pits, which became their mass graves. I have heard that the ground moved for days after the burial, for many were thrown into the pits and buried while wounded and still alive after the butchery. I was unable to find the mass grave of the women and children in the forest. Thus, 300 years of Jewish life and culture vanished forever without trace. Nothing remains of it today except our memories. Included was this note from the writer, now long dead:

"My yizkor saying"
My intention in making this map is that perhaps in the future

generations a grandchild or a great-grandchild will out of curiosity unfold this map. He may accidentally recognize a familiar name that he heard years ago in his parent's or grandparents' home. He will also read how and when the terrible Holocaust happened. It is my hope that this will remind him not to forget and not to forgive. [The Yizkor is a memorial service for family and friends to remember those who have died. It has taken on a modern meaning as an annual remembrance of victims of the Holocaust.—ed.]

Deeply affected by the story of the Holocaust in Dad's village, I prepared to visit Lithuania on a pilgrimage to my roots. The recounting of the aforementioned legend written by the long-dead stranger pays homage to the murdered families of Naumiestis, and I have decided to make sure that the Jews of Naumiestis will never be forgotten.

During the visit to Naumiestis in 1993, I found that not a vestige of Jewish life remains there despite three centuries of settlement. Almost without exception, the Jews in the village were murdered by the Nazis and their Lithuanian collaborators. I couldn't locate the various homes that appear in the map, and all that remains today of centuries of Jewish life in the village is a small marble plaque at the site of the former Jewish cemetery. The plaque stands over the mass grave of the entire male Jewish population—all those over the age of fourteen—and reads, "Here one thousand Soviet citizens were killed by the Nazis and the Lithuanian Fascists." Not a word mentions that the murdered citizens were all Jews. Moreover, I was unable to find a single tombstone among the weeds in the neglected patch of ground.

Ever since I was at the village I have found it impossible to reconcile the history of the mass murders with the appearance of the peaceful farming village and its inhabitants going about their daily tasks.

After leaving Lithuania at the end of the nineteenth century, my father never saw his parents again.

THE WHITE KAFFIR

In his early days in South Africa, Dad worked for a number of small country store owners and saved every penny he earned until he had a small amount of capital. After moving to Johannesburg and working for a movie distributor, he bought a nearby cinema that was for sale. It was in the time of the silent movies, and Dad employed a Mr. Cohen to sit below the screen and while watching the film play his violin: sad music for sad scenes and lively tunes for happy scenes. Mr. Cohen eventually scraped together enough money to buy a share in a small general store, the "OK Bazaars," which had been so named and started by my father. After some time it became a countrywide chain of large stores, and Mr. Cohen became a multimillionaire. Dad left the company shortly after it was formed. When he met Mr. Cohen at a cocktail party some thirty years later, Dad said to him, "You were not much of a violinist when you played for me!" His former employee replied, "It was my luck that I was a bad violinist, otherwise, I would probably still be playing for you in your cinema."

Dad sold his share in the OK Bazaars, made a good living

from the cinema, and after some years bought a share in a firm dealing with expedition and shipping, eventually buying control of the firm, which became the largest one of its kind. He continued to live modestly, working hard and became wealthy over the years by carefully saving his money. When my sister Selma asked him, "How did you make all that money?" his reply was typically short and simple. "I earned ten shillings a month and saved eight."

Years of self-denial did, indeed, contribute to his eventual wealth, and he continued throughout his life to spend a minimum on himself while at the same time donating large sums to charity and to people who were in trouble. He never spoke of these gifts, and we in the family only discovered them by chance if at all.

As the youngest of my brother and sisters, I spent much of my time alone, but there was one person to whom I was especially close, Jack Mahusho. Jack was of the Tswana tribe. He was in his thirties and good-natured. He had been employed by the family from long before I was born and was loved by all of us. There was, however, an apartheid barrier between him and our white family, which I never dared cross despite my love for him. The apartheid system operated at all levels and prevented contact and the growth of relations between the different races. Though there was a constant awareness of the gap between the whites and the blacks on a formal level, on the personal level close bonds often existed.

My mother was born in Yorkshire, England, and came to South Africa with her family at the age of six. Her whole background was English upper class, and she was a cultured woman with inborn ladylike manners. Unusual for a person with such an English background, she had a deep love for everything Jewish and especially for the nascent Yishuv (Jewish settlement) in Palestine. Her English education fused with her Jewish background and culture and made it possible for her to guide us constantly in our approach to life. Moreover her excellent command of English enabled her to assist us constantly with our formal studies. Not being a socialite, she was always on hand in the home to care for her children, and her interest in all our doings was fundamental to our upbringing. She disliked intensely any hint of ostentation and was unusually modest in her daily life. The functions she held in our home—musical recitals and talks given by the leaders of the Yishuv all occurred in an atmosphere of gentility and culture.

Besides my mother, Jack Mahusho was the one who attended to most of my needs. I was so close to him that often I refused to let him eat his meals alone in his room and insisted on sitting near him and eating mouthfuls of his *skaaf* (food) from his plate, usually a stew of sinewy meat in a tasty gravy of curry and cornmeal. On his weekend day off, I sometimes went into a tantrum if I were not allowed to accompany him to his home in the black township in Newlands. When I was thirteen, he was killed in a traffic accident. That was the first time I recall having broken down in uncontrollable weeping at the loss of a dear one.

St. Katherine's kindergarten in Johannesburg "for young ladies and young gentlemen" was my first school. The principal of the kindergarten was an elderly Englishwoman with a dried countenance. On one occasion when I was unruly and caused a girl to fall off the swing in the garden, she raged at me using what was in her eyes the worst possible epithet and one which gives a succinct view of the prevailing attitude toward our black compatriots at that time: "You are just a white Kaffir." The Kaffirs were a South African tribe.

My father was shorter than medium height with dark hair and fair skin, his hair always cropped very short in the Russian fashion. I recall as a child once having been taken to the barber by him and returning with an almost shaven head, which made me too ashamed to remove my hat for weeks except before going to bed. From then on I used every stratagem to avoid a visit to the barber with him for fear of another "Russian haircut."

The annual visits to the huge domed Wolmarans Street synagogue for Rosh Hashanah and Yom Kippur were my first exposure to Judaism. There were also Friday nights with the starched white tablecloth, the two candles, the Sabbath meal of gefilte fish and my brother Leon saying Kiddush. Each year we held the Passover Seder and read the ancient story of the Exodus in the *Hagadah*, the book that describes the Seder sequence, from beginning to end despite the fidgeting of the children impatiently awaiting the Pesach meal. I was invariably spellbound when my father counted out the ten plagues, accompanying each one by dipping a spoon into a glass of wine and depositing a drop on a large plate.

The break in the ceremony when the door to the outside was opened for the prophet Elijah to come in also fascinated us. The long table with the gleaming candlesticks added to the festive atmosphere. Both my parents, though intense in their belief in the ancient Jewish country Eretz Israel, and in their desire for a national homeland, were not religious although they zealously kept alive the Jewish traditions in their home. In other words, both were Zionists but secular in their beliefs. These, too, have been my own views since childhood.

Throughout my youth I remember we had visitors from Palestine, many of them well-known figures of Zionism and some of the stars of Hebrew theater and world-famous concert pianists and violinists. The great day for me was when Chaim Weizmann paid a visit to South Africa and came to our house to meet the notables of the community. A tall, distinguished man with a shining pate and small, cropped beard, he looked very much like Lenin. For me Weizmann was the "King of the Jews." I was seven years old and I begged to be allowed to sit next to him at dinner; my mother agreed and I sat next to him at the long table. Toward the end of the dinner, fruit was served. I remember that after I ate a large portion of grapes my mother told me that I had eaten enough. Downcast, I sat in silence at the long table. Chaim Weizmann quietly began to help himself to grapes and surreptitiously to hand them to me one by one under the table without my mother or the other guests knowing what was going on. I have to this day a sheet of paper with his signature and written above it "To Boris Senior with best love, Chaim Weizmann."

There is no doubt that Weizmann's role in modern political Zionism was seminal. I remember being brought up on the well-known story of his important breakthrough in the method of manufacturing acetone in World War I. I was told a very dramatized version of how his discovery helped win the war for Great Britain, and that as a mark of gratitude, King George V asked him what he could do for him.

His somewhat impertinent answer, "Your Majesty, please help my people get back their national homeland." A surely dramatized story that made an indelible impression on me. In Israel today, it is unusual to find even a small town that does not have a street named after Chaim Weizmann. He was a giant of the Zionist movement and was regarded with respect by the leaders of the world community in the first half of the twentieth century. Though born in what is today Belarus, he was an Anglophile, and the only criticism of him could be that he was too trusting of the British whom he so much admired. It is not surprising that Chaim Weizmann was elected the first president of the new State of Israel in 1948.

At that time, my parents began traveling to Europe and to Palestine regularly, at first by boat. In those days foreign travel was leisurely and carefully planned. I remember going with my mother to Thomas Cook's to arrange their journeys and being ushered into a large, gloomy office for a session to hear the plans, who would meet them at the boat train, where they would stay, and what vehicle would be there to take them to the various places. I would look with interest at my mother's steamer trunk in her bedroom and at the clothing on wooden hangers in both sides of the trunk, which would stand on end open like a book with corners reinforced with sturdy brass fittings. The trunk probably weighed some hundreds of kilos.

In the early 1930s, my parents began traveling by air, and we used to go early in the morning to Germiston Airport to bid them farewell. The first leg of the journey was in an Imperial Airways de Havilland Rapide twin-engine biplane with seven passengers and two pilots. My father, dressed in khaki shorts and shirt and a pith helmet, looked like an African explorer. As each passenger boarded the aircraft it tilted a little to one side. We stood close by on the grass as the pilot ran up the engines, and the airplane and its passengers inside shook and shivered. When the pilot taxied to the beginning of the grass field and took off over our heads, we tearfully waved good-bye.

The various legs of the flights of Imperial Airways were about three hours long and after each they landed for refueling. At the end of the day, they would retire to a nice hotel at their destination for a rest and a quiet evening. If the pilot saw some interesting wild game on the way, he would draw the attention of the passengers and circle the herd of elephants or giraffe or whatever. A few years later they would, after two days' flying, be transferred to a large four-engine Sunderland flying boat at Port Mozambique, with twelve passengers and a crew of five. The flying boat eventually landed in Palestine either on Lake Tiberias or on the Dead Sea. The flight took the better part of two weeks, and no one seemed to be in too much of a hurry. I have a clipping from a South African weekly that gives an idea of air travel in that period, with a heading on one page about my parents paying "a lightning visit to Palestine, there and back in one month." Now who had it better, the early travelers or us nowadays in the sleek jets?

THE LONELY TREE

The Sterkfontein caves, renowned for the traces of early prehistoric civilization they contain, are forty kilometers north of Johannesburg. Though we lived in Johannesburg, much of my youth was spent at Doornbosfontein, a farm we owned near the Sterkfontein. It is a large farm, and its name comes from a big Doornbos thornbush tree that stands in splendid isolation in a broad treeless landscape. From my early childhood, we called it "the lonely tree."

After establishing himself in South Africa, my father bought the farm for his sister and two brothers and their families as a home to live in when he brought them from Lithuania. It is huge—7,000 acres. The three immigrant families hailed from the small village in the distant Baltic country having had no experience in agriculture. They took to their new environment and occupation without difficulty, as has been the wont of Jews who so often have had to migrate from country to country. The district was populated by Afrikaans farmers, who looked on incredulously as the inexperienced Lithuanian immigrants, in their outlandish Russian dress with pale complexions, began to plant corn and reap crops with surprisingly good yields.

Despite knowing little English and not a word of Afrikaans, they were welcomed and were well treated by the God-fearing Afrikaner farmers who considered the Jews to be "the people of the Book." Probably the sympathetic attitude of the Afrikaans farmers to the Jews had its roots in the history of their Huguenot ancestors' flight from religious persecution in Europe in the seventeenth century.

The farmers had been accustomed to visits from time to time by a kind of Jewish immigrant called "smouses" in Afrikaans. They were traveling merchants who went from one isolated farm to another with a bag or two of articles for sale. The farmers were isolated from contact with their farmer compatriots because of the lack of facilities for communicating. They tended to rely on the traveling smouses to bring them news from other farmers. The peddlers were often put up for the night by the kind Afrikaners, but they had not expected to see them working beside them as farmers. My father always spoke well of them and of the Afrikaners and their welcoming attitude to newcomers.

Most of the road from Johannesburg to Doornbosfontein is tarred, but the last ten kilometers consists of dirt roads winding through low hills covered in dry brown grass and fields of corn, the staple food of most black South Africans. As these roads pass through farms, there are gates every few kilometers, and if one throws a coin to the Picannins who are nearby, they open and close the gate with a winning smile. After leaving the tarred road, four farms are passed in this way, the last belonging to the family of Dolf de la Rey, descendant of the famed Afrikaner general of the Boer War.

Our homestead at Doornbosfontein was near the farm entrance and consisted of one large ancient farmhouse and another smaller building composed of what is known as *rondavels*. These are unique to South Africa and are circular structures with roofs made of thatch, the interior construction exposed and consisting of long poles of poplar wood, which support the thatch. The poles end in a conical top, the whole making a pleasant appearance with the bundles of thatch forming attractive ceilings especially in the soft light of paraffin lamps. The thick walls are made of bricks and plaster painted white inside and out, and inside there is always the peculiar but pleasant smell of thatch. Apart from some danger of fire, there can be no better form of roof, cool in summer and warm in winter.

The atmosphere of the veld pervades everything. At Doornbosfontein, we always felt close to nature. It is usually bone dry, but in the summer after a rain shower, the air is suffused with the wonderful pungent odor of dry earth wet by rain. The rain comes in the early afternoon, preceded by vast buildups of towering cumulus storm clouds, which invariably give birth to wild storms. When we sought shelter in our *rondavels*, the rain could not even be heard through the thick thatch, and we felt cozy and safe. Outside, the veld stretched as far as the eye could see, the parched earth drinking in the life-giving fluid from the heavens, the dry cracks in the earth healing as the rain smoothed the ravages of the burning sun.

A dam at the end of a stream supplied water of good quality. There was no telephone or electricity at Doornbosfontein, and the nearest telephone and post office were at Orient rail station, seven kilometers away. Part of the farm is in a mountain range. It was a magnet for us children because of its streams, steep valleys, and populations of buck, porcupines, monkeys, and other wild life. The mountains were reached by the whole family in a large ox-wagon drawn by sixteen slow-moving oxen, led by the black *voorloper* pacing along slowly at their head. On arrival at the "kloof" as we called it, the *voorloper* would tighten brakes made of large blocks of wood pressed against the rear wheels. We would start down the incline, and I remember the fear I felt during the steep descent behind the bellowing oxen. It is hard to believe that in the eighteenth century the mass movement of the Afrikaners from the Cape to the far north a thousand miles away was made in the same kind of wagon.

The farm was basic, without electricity. We made do with Primus stoves for cooking, and the kerosene lamps at night lent a cozy atmosphere to the rondavel. Meals were simple. A profusion of salads, vegetables, and white cheese made by my mother by hanging cloth bags of sour cream on a tree, from which we could see the whey dripping. My mother loved the simplicity of life at the farm and refused to introduce modern gadgets. Even our water was drawn from the dam nearby and carried to the *rondavels*.

Our relatives eventually decided that life on a farm in South Africa was not for them and left Doornbosfontein for the city. My father arranged with various tenant farmers to live in and run the farm. They lived in the big house with their families while we kept the rondavels for weekends and vacations. The farmers were mostly Afrikaans, many down on their luck from drinking, and were a continual source of trouble. The black workers were more-permanent residents at the farm and lived in a village they had built at one end of the farm. They were entirely independent, provided they gave us one-third of whatever crops they grew on the land near the village. They had their own hierarchy, and their church nearby was on our land, its exterior walls gaily decorated in African fashion. I remember the great respect tinged with some fear we children accorded their old headman Oom Paul with his one blind eye.

In the early 1930s, my father, always a keen Zionist, offered Doornbosfontein as a training farm for prospective migrants to Palestine, and there were groups of young men living there studying agriculture as part of the Hechalutz movement. It was doubtless strange for the Afrikaner farmers in the area to visit the large central rondavel, which had been turned into a dining room and lecture hall, to see the slogans about the Promised Land posted on the walls in Hebrew. Not a few of the kibbutzniks in Israel today must remember their months of training in farming at Doornbosfontein. Years later, to all our regret, the farm was sold and has since become a large cattle ranch.

Hilton

When I was twelve years old, I was sent to Hilton College, a boarding school 700 kilometers from Johannesburg. The train journey took a night and half a day with carriages for girls going to schools in the same area. We were all homesick and excited, and after nightfall we visited the girls' carriages. In time, the school authorities understood what was going on during the overnight journey, and they locked the corridor leading to the girls' carriages. That did not stop us, for we climbed out of our windows and made our way by crawling along outside the carriages to enter the girls' side. The train was all the while hurtling through the night at high speed.

In the morning the train continued to speed through the flat Transvaal landscape halting momentarily at dry "dorps," where barefoot black youths, mucous dribbling from their noses, stood in the cold near the tracks with their hands stretched out begging. When the train pulled into the station at Hilton Road after lunch the following day, we traveled by car through the forests and had our first sight of the beautiful school, situated in its own estate of thousands of acres of forest and mountains with wide rivers coursing through it. The buildings were in the Cape Dutch style, snow-white with black roofs and gables at the ends of the buildings surrounded by well-tended lawns.

Each dormitory had twenty beds, not one of which had even a shelf or night cupboard for one's own personal belongings next to it, creating a feeling of impersonality for us. The dormitories with their iron bedsteads looked like soldiers' barracks. Showers were communal, first thing in the morning and in the afternoon after sport. No hot water was available in the showers probably because of belief that cold showers reduce libido. It was strange to be in the shower room early on a winter morning, freezing and crowded with boys who ran one by one into the shower, gasping loudly and rubbing themselves furiously as the cold water streamed onto their sleepy bodies. Hot baths were allowed for ten minutes twice a week, strictly according to a timetable listing names and times of bathing.

Daily routine meant rising at 0630, and after a compulsory ice-cold shower, standing in line to get a mug of cocoa and one slice of bread and jam before chapel for the morning service. As it is an Anglican school, Jews and Roman Catholics were exempted from chapel and went to the library to await the end of the service.

On that first day, still wearing my Hilton tie, I removed my jacket and took a walk around the school. As I passed in front of the main building, a teacher beckoned me over to him and said coldly, "I think it might be preferable if you

were not to walk around the school without your jacket."
That was my first encounter with the school establishment.
All the hopes and expectations of the great adventure of becoming a schoolboy at Hilton gave way in an instant to a
sense of feeling an outcast in a stiff and hostile environment.
In general, the atmosphere at the school was suffused with a
certain coldness, which probably came from the rigid English public-school rules and customs. In the first few days
of my stay at Hilton, I was very homesick and had a desolate
feeling when something reminded me of my home and its
warmth and coziness.

Discipline at Hilton was strict in all respects, and punishment was meted out for all transgressions. More serious
overstepping of the rules meant corporal punishment. The
prefects enjoyed various privileges and were allowed to cane
any boy who overstepped rules. In short, discipline at the
school was harsh, but there were rewards for those boys
who obeyed the draconian rules.

One of the features of Hilton was the practice of being
referred to only by your surname. First names were used by
one's closest friends only. If there was more than one boy
with the same name, you were given a title, which would be
for example Smith Major, Minor, or Tertius. This practice
is followed at English public schools, and it created for me
an atmosphere of coldness and impersonality. Another rig-
orously followed custom of the English public school at Hilton was fagging. Any boy who had been at the school for
two years became an "old poop," which entitled him to employ any of the "new poops" to fetch and carry for him, to
brush his blazer and polish his shoes.

Morning chapel was followed by study in the classrooms, after which we had breakfast in the large dining hall. The walls were covered in wooden panels, each dedicated to the various generations of families. I noted that many of the panels contained names ranging from grandfather to father and then to son, with the dates of attendance at Hilton, in some cases extending for nearly a hundred years. Apart from the two teachers of Afrikaans, the masters were all graduates of Oxford or Cambridge, and the influence of the British Empire, at that time the paramount power in the world, pervaded the school environment. In addition to the regular syllabus, there was an emphasis on classical subjects such as Latin, which I studied for five years, and classical Greek.

Some minor anti-Semitism existed among the boys, but it never amounted to more than a remark. The teachers never showed a hint of it. Whether by chance or by intent, there were only a handful of Jewish boys at Hilton.

Food was wholesome and good, preceded by grace at long tables. Seating was always unchanged, each house or dormitory at its own separate table. Care was taken to ensure that whenever pork or bacon was served for meals, other meat was available for the seven or eight Jewish boys among the 230 boys at the school. Apart from the fact that we did not eat any meat originating from a pig, and did not go to chapel, there was no difference between the pupils, and no discrimination of any kind. Knowing what existed in much of "enlightened" Europe at that time, South Africa can be viewed only, though admittedly from the standpoint of a white citizen, as a haven of decency.

Probably the complete lack of bias between the members

of the white population had its roots in the need for solidarity among the whites in face of the perceived danger of being overwhelmed by the large black majority in South Africa.

In Johannesburg, the pleasant environment for white South Africans in the 1940s belied the tensions resulting from the laws of apartheid as the whites were to a great extent shielded from the iniquities of the laws. Certainly, the fact that I was so protected from what happened in my own society during my youth was a contributory factor to the shock I experienced when I learned after the war about the death camps of Nazi Germany, for I had experienced virtually no anti-Semitism.

There is also a curious affinity between the Afrikaners and the Jews. Many of them see a parallel between the rebirth of Israel with its struggle for survival and their own efforts to exist as a tiny minority in a sea of blacks. There are also traces of the Calvinist belief among the original Huguenot and old Dutch settlers that their mission was to Christianize and uplift the indigenous peoples in southern Africa.

When I left Hilton by train for the last time, I felt satisfaction at leaving school. However, the great expectations of facing the next hurdle of life were tinged with some uneasiness at leaving the safe cocoon of our protected school routine. Though we were all attached to Hilton, it was a relief to be freed of the strict discipline. I still recall the deep comradeship, which can come only from shared experiences and from living together throughout long months.

CHAPTER THREE

War

WINGS PARADE

THE news of the fall of France in June 1940 reached me one late afternoon on a gray, depressing day. After reading so much about the Allied armies and the great French commanding generals Weygand and Gamelin, I was shocked by their humiliating defeat. I began to fear that we were lost and that our seemingly known and secure world would henceforth be run by Hitler and his henchmen. It felt like the beginning of the end of life as we knew it.

After finishing school, all I wanted to do was to join the South African Air Force, learn to fly, and get into a fighter squadron as quickly as possible. In South Africa in World War II, there was no conscription, but until age twenty-one, parental permission was required for volunteers. As my older brother Leon was already in the air force, I agreed to my parents' request to wait for one year before joining up, and I began studies at the university in Johannesburg.

In the midst of the war and with climactic events happening daily in the various theaters of war, I found it well-nigh impossible to do anything but think about the war. Only with difficulty was I able to wait my turn to enlist. With the war dominating my thoughts and everything I did, campus life seemed tame, and as most of us felt the same, we took part in campus life only half-heartedly.

Leon was a flight instructor, and he realized that I was serious about joining the air force. Leon arranged for me to be taken up with one of his associates at the flying school. Probably on Leon's instructions, he put the Hawker Hart biplane through its paces in aerobatics to frighten me off flying. The fully aerobatic biplane enabled the instructor to throw it around the sky and fly it inverted; of course, it had the opposite effect for I couldn't wait to start flying.

After passing exhaustive medical examinations, I went to the Lyttleton base of the South African Air Force for aptitude tests. I failed the aptitude test as a pilot, and after refusing under any circumstances to relinquish my dream of piloting by agreeing to become an air gunner or navigator, I realized that I had to find some other way of getting on a pilot's course. I had heard that it was possible to join the Chinese Air Force of General Chiang Kai-shek, so I paid a visit to the Chinese consulate in Johannesburg. They were polite but said that I would have to make my own way to the provisional capital in Chungking to offer my services. In the middle of the war this was clearly not feasible, so I went to Rhodesia to try to gain acceptance by the Royal Air Force, Rhodesia being a British colony.

Upon arrival in Salisbury, I went to the RAF recruiting center only to be told that South Africans were not accepted and that the only option for me was to return and join the South African Air Force.

At my wits end, I next went to see the Belgian consul in Salisbury to try to get accepted to the Belgian Air Force, for pilots from the Belgian Congo were training with the South African Air Force. The Belgian consul informed me that they, too, did not accept anyone from South Africa. Sad and disheartened I decided to return to Johannesburg and to apply to enlist as a navigator.

I boarded the train back to Johannesburg just before dusk and went to the dining car for dinner. By chance, my partner at the table was a personable young Greek Air Force lieutenant, who proudly wore a brand new pair of wings, which he had gained after completing his flying training in Rhodesia. Over dinner, he patiently answered my questions about his flying course. Realizing that he was far from his home and feeling lonely, I invited him to spend time with us in Johannesburg before he continued to the Middle East to join a Greek Air Force squadron. His name was George Lagodimus, and we promised to meet again when the war was over. Our next meeting turned out to be one neither of us could have foreseen.

Eventually, the South African Air Force, perhaps impressed by my persistence, relented when I reappeared, and they accepted me for pilot training. The initial training was at Lyttleton, a cold and deserted-looking camp in the Transvaal veld near Pretoria. Our welcome was not encouraging for it was the habit of the cadets to shout "Go home!" as soon as a bunch of new recruits appeared.

The discipline at the initial training base was harsh. The

commander of the base was a colonel. He had a large black dog that wore a major's crown on his collar, and we had to salute the dog every time we passed him. We all took this quirk in good humor, having been told that when saluting an officer we were saluting not the wearer of the rank but the King's commission.

There were a mixed bunch of would-be pilots in our course: Afrikaners, Englishmen, and a few Jews. Food on the base was plentiful, but the timing of some meals was strange for when we got up in the early morning at 0430, we were often served either steak or mutton chops and mashed potatoes, a little hard to cope with at that time of day. There was much drinking by the cadets at the bar of Polly's hotel in Pretoria, making our way back to the camp in the early hours of the morning.

In time we were sent on a gliding course. The first time I saw the elementary instruction glider, I was surprised to see that it consisted of a bulky wing with a fuselage, which was an open-frame construction without any covering. It looked to me as though it was a cut-down model made to show us how it was constructed. The instructor was puzzled when I quite innocently asked when we would see the real glider.

We were strapped into this contraption and towed along at high speed by a cable attached to a winch. We released ourselves from the cable at 800 feet. We were encouraged to sing when up in the air in order to help us relax, and it was amusing to hear a pupil singing gaily high above us.

The next step in pursuit of my wings was at the elementary flying school, near the small town of Potchefstroom in the Transvaal, to complete seventy-five hours on the yellow de Havilland Tiger Moth biplanes. They were fairly difficult aircraft to fly accurately and were therefore good for training. The flights in these fully aerobatic trainers with their two open cockpits in tandem for the instructor and the pupil were exhilarating. They were old but reliable airplanes and even some of the maneuvers, which demanded that I be suspended upside down with my head and part of my upper body hanging out in the slipstream, did not worry me. The Tiger Moths were constructed of aluminum tubing covered in fabric, which even at that time seemed old-fashioned.

My instructor was named Cohen, and a friend in the course ahead of me who was also Cohen's pupil complained bitterly about his behavior. Was this coincidence, or was someone arranging for the "Jew boys" to be lumped together? Whatever the reason, we both attained our wings despite our instructor. Cohen was awful. Whether his nerves were shot from a tour of operations in a squadron in North Africa or from instructing I don't know. He screamed and swore at his pupils, and would get so enraged when we made mistakes that he would sometimes undo his harness and stand up in the front cockpit with his control column in his fist threatening to brain us. One of the senior pupil pilots, who had also had the misfortune to be assigned to him, had secretly bent the pins in Cohen's parachute and planned to do a slow roll when he got out of his harness, hoping to get rid of him for good. Of course, he chickened out.

Cohen did not exactly encourage his pupils, but I managed to be assigned to another instructor who was a relief after him. After my dual time of seven and a half hours of circuits and bumps, the instructor removed his stick and said, "Off you go now. You are going to be all right."

Though it was an achievement, a landmark in my life, my first solo was a bit of an anticlimax for I felt no great anxiety when I was left on my own. I just flew the Tiger Moth as I had been taught to do, and the aircraft responded as expected. The great joy came to me in the solo flights that followed later, and I was delighted to be up in the sky alone.

Shortly after that we began aerobatics, and I quickly learned that the Tiger is a most difficult aircraft in which to perform a good slow roll. It was not easy to stop the nose straying to the left or right of its initial position and to keep exactly the same height. All aerobatics are wisely preceded by 360-degree steep turns to ensure that the area is free of other aircraft. On my first attempt to do solo aerobatics, I remained inverted during one of the maneuvers for too long. My engine cut and I was hard put to get it restarted again. Fortunately, I succeeded. In general, aerobatics, which included loops, slow rolls, and the much-easier barrel rolls, stall turns, and rolls off the top, were a great pleasure. Aerobatics teaches you how to maintain complete command of your craft in any attitude and gives confidence in your ability to handle the airplane.

MISCHIEF IN THE AIR

After a hundred hours of advanced flying instruction, I had my first night flight. At night, the air is usually smooth. To be up on your own, high above the lights on the ground, gives a feeling of being divorced from the earth and your environment while you are suspended in an immense black vault with no beginning and no end. The muted glow of the instrument panel lends a quietness and intimacy to the mood in the cockpit as you glance from the instruments to the world outside. All sounds sound different at night, more muted, and even voices were more subdued. I always felt more at one with my aircraft at night than during the day. The conclusion to a night flight invariably gave me a sense of achievement, and the gooseneck paraffin flares on the side of the runway lent an unusually dramatic atmosphere to our familiar environment.

The Harvard (AT-6) trainers we graduated to were much superior to the Tiger Moths in elementary flying school, and this was the reason I was nearly washed out of the course. Shortly before the great day of the wings parade, we had to make a long solo, triangular cross-country flight. During the flight, I spotted a yellow Tiger Moth flying on a course well below me across my track. Only one of the cockpits was occupied, and assuming that it was a junior pupil on a cross-country flight from the elementary flying school, I could not resist buzzing him repeatedly, thinking that I was showing the sprog some ace flying. I was a little surprised that he did not seem fazed by the mock attacks I made on him, merely continuing to fly a straight and level course. I saw his head in the open cockpit probably giving me a baleful look as I dived down on him at high speed from above. After attending funerals at flying school, I have come to the conclusion that the most dangerous period in one's flying career is after solo and completing a number of hours at flying school. That is when you are convinced that you are probably the hottest pilot around.

About a week later, I was called into the base commander's office and was told that I had been seen dangerously buzzing a Tiger Moth flown by no less than a colonel who was the aide-de-camp to Prime Minister General Smuts. He had made a note of the number of my aircraft and reported me. A court martial followed, ending in a sentence of ten days detention. I remember standing at attention facing the judge in my short pants and struggling to keep my knees from knocking together. I spent the time in a cell in a military police post. One memory that I have of that confinement was that the door to my cell had no handle on the inside making me feel completely cut off from the world outside. It occurred to me that it would be very unpleasant should a fire break out. However, the most important point was that I was not going to be washed out of my flying course and merely faced a delay of one course, about six weeks.

Finally, the great day came for the wings parade. It was already getting late in the war, and I was concerned that the fighting might end before I could get to a fighter squadron. After rehearsals for the wings parade, we were at last ready for the ceremony, which came after eighteen months of hard training, dropping off, by the way, three-quarters of those who had appeared at the beginning for the aircrew medical and aptitude tests.

My mother and my brother came for the ceremony, and Leon and his wife gave me a silver identity bracelet wishing me luck. As it turned out, we both needed luck in the final months of the war, for Leon never made it and I very nearly didn't either. I was awarded the rank of second lieutenant, and though I wore my rank proudly, it was nothing compared to the wings on my left breast. I was graded as a fighter pilot, a target for which I had aimed for years.

KITTYHAWK

From the advanced flying school, I was posted to the Operational Training Unit (OTU) at Waterkloof near Pretoria. Here we were treated as officers and gentlemen, having rooms with hot and cold water. We ate in a mess at separate tables with food served by waiters. By this time I had bought a small secondhand Morris Eight car and could drive to Johannesburg on weekends and often again during the week.

At Waterkloof I flew my first fighter aircraft, the P-40 Kittyhawk and the Hawker Hurricane. The high performance of these fighters was exhilarating after having flown only training aircraft. As they were single-seat aircraft, we immediately went solo with surprisingly few mishaps.

To me the ex–Battle of Britain Hurricanes faded quickly into the background after flying the Kittyhawk. This aircraft seemed to kindle in me, and I believe in most of us, a blind faith and affection. Being American it had most of the human comforts that could be crammed into a restricted fighter cockpit, including enough leg room and ample space on either side of the pilot's seat. The canopy also could be rolled back to leave a comfortably large aperture when entering or leaving the cockpit. The Kittyhawk was a beautiful airplane with classic lines. The pointed nose, painted like the gaping maw of a shark, and the large tail made her stand out among other fighters. The history of her almost identical sister aircraft, the Tomahawk, used by China in the war against the Japanese invader in 1941–42 by General Chennault's Flying Tigers, lent a special aura to the Kitty.

OTU was great, and here I experienced my first real blackouts when pulling out of high-speed dives. But by far the best part was the dogfight training. We were encouraged to practice by selecting a partner and entering into a mad pursuit of one another, twisting and turning, diving and zooming in the skies. This routine, made more precarious by the large number of dogfights in the same general area, did sometimes claim victims.

One of our instructors was Lieutenant Robinson, an experienced fighter pilot. Despite his English-sounding name, he was a dyed-in-the-wool, wiry Afrikaner who, during his tour of operations in North Africa, had been shot down in error by a P-38 Lightning flown by a U.S. pilot who was new to operations in the area and mistook him for a Jerry. Poor Robbie, after having survived a tough tour of operations in North Africa, was killed when an OTU pupil collided with him over Pretoria, his hometown.

After the OTU course, we received embarkation leave before departing for Egypt to await a transfer to a squadron. Leon had just completed his third tour of instructing at various training bases in South Africa and got a posting to an OTU in Palestine before transferring to a bomber squadron.

I gave up my embarkation leave to leave for Cairo in the same aircraft with him.

EGYPT

The flight north to Egypt took five days in a Dakota [C-47] with four night stops: northern Rhodesia, Tanganyika, Kenya, and the Sudan. Everywhere, Leon and I were looked upon as unique—two brothers wearing wings and flying together to a theater of war. We were more than once asked to sign a visitor's book. The long flight gave us views of Africa's changing landscape, changes only in degree, for it was just different kinds of bush all the way up to the Sudan. Thereafter, the expanse of desert and sand was broken only by the life-giving Nile, which kept us company for most of the time after Lake Victoria. During the long leg of 2,000 kilometers through the Sudan, the forsaken towns of Juba and Malakal were the only signs of civilization in the endless wastes of the desert.

In Khartoum we stayed at the Grand Hotel for the night, and we noted with surprise the tall, jet-black Sudanese waiters dressed in white galabiyas with a red sash and red tarbush headgear. I was introduced to the British way of coping with the heat of Sudan using many huge ceiling fans in the lounge of the hotel. In Khartoum I had my first experience of life in an outpost of the British Empire. That was in a nightclub on a roof, replete with a cabaret and tired girls from France, who were obviously at their last stop before moving to an older profession. After Khartoum we stopped to refuel in Wadi Halfa, a dry desert town in the middle of featureless sandy wastes. A blast of heat like a furnace seared our faces as the door of the Dakota was opened.

We eventually arrived in Cairo and headed to the air force camp at Almaza, some miles beyond the eastern outskirts of Cairo in the desert, a flat and uninteresting scene. We were housed in tents in the sand, and here we made our acquaintance with the huge Egyptian onions, which were fed to us interminably and which served also as the raw material for Stella beer. Commuting to the city from Almaza was by fast electric train, which looked like a line of oversized city trams. On the half-hour journey we got a good view of Cairo. The filth and backwardness was a shock. The people of the city used the gutters on the roads as toilets. No one paid attention as men in their galabiyas and women in their shifts simply squatted, deftly did their bodily functions, then got up and walked off.

Our first confrontation with the families in the poorer quarters was when, through the train windows, we were puzzled at seeing babies with huge black eyes. On closer scrutiny we found that the large black patches were swarms of flies! The mothers holding the babies appeared to be oblivious to the danger of infection, and this is probably one of the reasons for the great amount of trachoma in the country.

The Heliopolis tram terminus was where we alighted in downtown Cairo and where young boys waited to beg or sell us trinkets. I fancied a short leather cane, which was the fashion among British officers at the time. I had seen one locally made that had a long sword cunningly hidden inside. A quick glance from me at one of the canes was enough to reveal my interest, and the boy asked for five Egyptian pounds. I had already learned not to react, and he followed me from place to place, reducing the price from time to time while I remained silent. After a week of his waiting for me at the terminus, we finally did the deal at thirty-five piastre, less than half a pound. Apart from their prices and shameless bargaining, however, the Egyptian boys were harmless and charming.

Masses of people everywhere and the nagging vendors of everything from "nice French girl, very sanitary, very hygienic, sir" to perfume, ivory chess sets, and anything one could possibly think of were novel at first but became tiresome. I found it hard to avoid their pestering until an old Cairo hand suggested that when they name a price, to offer a much higher one. That proved to be the only way to be free of them for they would slouch off saying *madjnum* (crazy).

I pitied the boys of seven and eight years, who spent their lives in the Mouski Bazaar making silver-filigree jewelry. When we traveled by train, we saw there was an ongoing battle between the railway police and the Egyptian boys, who rode on the roof without paying. Shoe-shine boys accosted us constantly, and if we refused their services when in a quiet street, they splashed our shoes with mud from tins they carried as marketing tools.

Cairo is alluring with its Arab music, the men's flowing robes, shops open until 11 o'clock at night, and trams like floating masses of humanity, with passengers clinging like locusts to the outside of the car in such numbers that the vehicles are entirely hidden beneath them.

The South African Officer's Club was in the center of the city and a convenient place for us to spend time; it was a microcosm of the life of pampered South African whites with Sudanese staff who saw to your every comfort from the moment you walked in, running your bath, pressing your uniform, and serving drinks and food.

There was little nightlife, only the Badia Cabaret with young attractive girls dancing on the stage, covered from tip to toe in gold paint. They were chaperoned by their mothers, and my request to meet one such beauty for a drink or a meal was firmly rejected by her mother who speedily interposed herself between us. It was also strange to see Egyptian men from villages and strange to the city and its nightlife getting excited by the girls' dancing and rushing forward to the stage while blowing passionate kisses.

In perfume shops the merchants seated us like maharajas and served Turkish coffee while we were induced to sample every fragrance in the shop. Many of us fell for the slick marketing trick, and our girls at home received small bottles of perfume often containing only colored tea.

The color and the vibrancy of the great city with its millions was overwhelming for someone like me, shielded from the masses by the orderly society of South Africa with its smaller cities. I was also separated by the race barriers from the poorer blacks, their trials and tribulations hidden from us so completely that we led a sheltered and, in retrospect, unreal existence.

To be suddenly thrown into the maelstrom of Cairo's

millions who tend to live a large part of their lives in the street was a shock to us, and we were troubled by the adversities of the people among whom we were stationed. Too often, however, we didn't heed their situation and were contemptuous of what appeared to be their strange, sometimes even reprehensible, customs and morals. On one occasion, though, I visited the home of a girl who belonged to a wealthy family in the Cairo suburb of Zamalek and found that they had nothing to learn about luxurious living from the South African well-to-do classes. The rich and fashionable lifestyle in the luxurious villas in Zamalek and Gezireh were in stark contrast to the abject poverty and filth elsewhere in Cairo.

SPITFIRE

After waiting impatiently in Cairo for news of an assignment to a fighter squadron, I was posted to a conversion course on Spitfires in Fayid, near the Suez Canal. There, I made my acquaintance with the legendary Spitfire. The Spit VB with the clipped wingtips was a small aircraft with a cockpit looking like an afterthought, everything cramped and seemingly added at the last minute. For example, the handle for retracting the undercarriage was on the right side of the cockpit down near the floor in an inconvenient place below your leg, demanding a change of hands at the critical times of takeoff and landing. The flying characteristics were superb, however, and the performance of the Spitfire was untouched in many respects by any fighter at the time. It had a rate of climb that surpassed anything in the air and could outmaneuver any fighter of the time. Its many idiosyncrasies demanded that it be treated with extreme delicacy, and it could be compared only to a dainty female of great beauty and sensitivity.

Because of its very long nose and narrow undercarriage, landing was not easy, for it necessitated a curving turn in the last phase of the approach. Otherwise, it was difficult to see the runway. This curving turn had to be maintained until just before touchdown, not an easy maneuver at that stage of the flight. The Spitfire had an elliptical wing, which was also unique. Ground attack roles were a different matter. Though it was used more often for those missions toward the end of the war in Europe, it suffered greatly, like other water-cooled engine fighters, from anti-aircraft fire if hit anywhere under the belly where the unprotected Glycol coolant flowed.

One of the more irksome features was the inability to open the canopy at any speed above 120 miles per hour. My first flight was alarming, for I hadn't noted this feature in the pilot's manual, and while coming in for my first landing at Fayid, I tried to open the canopy on the approach. All my efforts were to no avail leaving me close to panic with the feeling that I was trapped in the cockpit. I should, of course, have paid more attention to the instructions before that first flight.

After Fayid I had the choice of either waiting in Cairo for a posting to a squadron or, in the meantime, ferrying Corsair fighters from Egypt to India. Though I was interested in flying this gull-wing radial-engine navy fighter, with some hesitation because of my interest in seeing India, I chose the former option. I feared that a vacancy might come in a squadron, and I might miss it.

In the end, my hunch proved to be right, for soon I got a posting to 250 (Sudan) Squadron of the Desert Air Force in Italy. As it was a Royal Air Force squadron, I was to be seconded from the South African Air Force to the RAF. Within a few days I flew to Bari in southern Italy.

ITALY

Bari was my first stop in Italy, and for me, it was a disappointing first view of Europe. In late September 1944, at the onset of a freezing winter, the rains created mud and filth everywhere. The towns under the Allied occupation looked gray and suffering with their shuttered windows and bolted doors. Many of the buildings were crumbling from the persistent rain.

The cities were sad reflections of what they had once been. They were crowded with aimless groups of poorly clad men and women in wooden clogs. The dimly lit shops offered little, while the women engaged in the never-ending barter of eggs for military issue cigarettes.

Only in the largest cities was there some nightlife, with officers and other ranks defying military orders and fraternizing with the local Italian population. Some of the cabarets I later visited in Rome were of an unexpectedly high standard with the acrobats and dancers bravely trying to preserve their artistic level and their dignity amid the drunkenness and the groping. The servicemen were looking for sex but were often also seeking tenderness, sentimentality, and romance. The opera was crowded. There were jarring cheers and applause bursting from the masses in uniform at the appearance of a comely singer. A raucous disclaim of talent. The nightclubs were awash with cheap asti spumante white wine, and the performers tried to put on a good front in the atmosphere of darkness, tobacco smoke, and drunkenness.

In Italy I found the American servicemen very different from the British. Usually, Allied troops got on well, but once in Rome during a night's frivolity in a large nightclub, a drunken American infantry major rushed from table to table, scowling threateningly as he asked all the RAF pilots if they had been flying a P-47 Thunderbolt in operations anywhere near the front line on the Adriatic side of Italy. I soon discovered that he was searching for fighter-bombers with markings different from those of the United States, which had mistakenly attacked his unit, killing some of his comrades. Fortunately I had been flying P-51s and P-40s, and I prefer not to think of what might have happened to me had I told him that I was flying P-47s.

I walked back to the hotel with two RAF men, and I recall my exaggerated praise of Britain alone in its stand against Hitler for so long and my disappointment with the United States for having entered the war so late. There is no doubt that had it not been for Britain in its stand in the early days of the war, the world would have fallen to the Nazis. Neither can there be doubt that without the power and industrial strength of the United States, Britain and her allies would not have been able to withstand the forces of Nazi evil.

I was attracted by the relaxed American approach to life. The Americans seemed hooked on our bully beef, which we could not look at after a few months. We often swapped it for their Spam. I encountered examples of the Americans' easy-going attitude when I met a U.S. pilot watching a Spitfire in which I was to take off. We discussed the relative merits of my Spit and his twin-engine P-38, which I admired. He said, "You let me fly your Spitfire and I'll let you fly my P-38," and he meant it. Also on one occasion, I hitched a ride in a U.S. C-47 from Rome to Naples, entirely without formal listing or permission, the pilot just saying "Sure thing, hop in and I'll drop you off in Naples."

On arrival, I was billeted temporarily in a villa high in the Vomero. The villa was exquisite and peaceful, and below in the distance was a beautiful view of Naples and its bay. Down below but much nearer was the ugliness of the city with its corrupting hunger and despair.

PERUGIA

Before a posting to 250 Squadron, I was sent to the Refresher Flying Unit (RFU) at Perugia to become familiar with the fighter aircraft we were to fly on missions and to get accustomed to flying in the European winter. The unit was at a strip between Perugia and Assisi, and we were lodged in a large farmhouse in which the owner, squire of the area, was ill and near death. The farmhouse was a pleasant building on two floors and was an impressive, beautiful home for the family that had owned it. However, by the time we moved into it as quarters, it looked like what it was—billets for serving personnel, unkempt and showing the effects of being a transit camp.

In the midst of a freezing winter, heating became our main preoccupation. In sub-zero temperatures, we had no heating of any kind, not even hot water. In the officers' mess, the margarine for spreading on bread was frozen stiff. Our first priority was to heat our bedrooms and to get hot water. After moving into the rooms on the second floor, we broke holes in the exterior walls of our rooms, inserted makeshift chimneys, and constructed heating units made of forty-four-gallon drums with a copper pipe. We hammered the end so that a small jet of high-octane aircraft gasoline could be squirted into the drum.

We arranged flat burner trays below this outlet and fed in the high-octane fuel by gravity. This gave a blue flame with copious amounts of heat. We got ourselves so well organized that we began to feel very much at home. All went well except for the fact that our knocking and hammering upset the owner on his deathbed, and his daughter begged us to desist during the night.

While at Perugia a lively commerce began with the local Italian farm girls who brought us fresh eggs, which we paid for at the rate of ten cigarettes for one egg. The Italians had little trust in the Allied Military Government (AMGOT) money with which we had been issued. Very welcome mail from home began arriving for the first time on a regular basis. I had been given a strange address for my mother to use: care of the Director of Personnel, SAAF Headquarters, Villa Victoria, Cairo. Surprisingly, there were regular deliveries every week or two.

In Perugia I met Tony Wills, a South African from Natal, who had gotten his wings at about the same time as me and also had a posting to 250 Squadron. He had blond hair and a blond moustache and was of a quiet disposition, rarely getting hassled by anything. We struck up an immediate friendship and became inseparable. I knew that he intended to become a teacher after completing his war service, and as he was a dyed-in-the-wool Natal resident of English stock, we found that my background of many years' schooling in Natal enabled us to have much in common. After the RFU we were sent to the squadron on the same day. In time we were to team up and fly many missions together.

FIRST MISSION

I arrived at the squadron while it was billeted in a modern block of flats in the center of the small town of Fano on the Adriatic coast. We were three to a room, with better conditions than I had expected. Batmen saw to our laundry, cooking, and cleaning. Our pilots were a mixed bunch from various parts of the British Empire. In addition to the English pilots we had South Africans, Canadians, and Australians, and we all got on well.

Willie and I arrived late at night from the refresher course in Perugia and stumbled into the building in the dark, insecure and uptight at the future awaiting us in an operational fighter squadron near the front line. A sergeant directed us to our sleeping quarters in one of the first-floor flats. When we heard raucous shouting and cursing, we went down the stairs and found a wild party was in progress in the cellar below. Alcohol was flowing, and everyone seemed to be having a great time while shooting at the ceiling and at the walls from the pilots' issue revolvers.

Conspicuous among the drunken pilots was one with his shirt hanging out, black rings around his eyes and a wild look. He was called Robbie. He was deputy squadron commander and had flown close to the 200 mission hours required to complete his tour of operations before going home. He had a fine record, but it was clear that he was almost at breaking point, something that happened to many at that stage of their operational career. I had the opportunity to fly with Robbie on a number of missions, and his handling of the squadron was responsible and skilled. His behavior at the party was his way of letting off steam and did not impair his operational competence.

When I asked one of the pilots what the occasion was for the party, he off-handedly said, "We lost two more pilots over Padua this morning." I asked if this was unusual. The laconic reply was, "No, we lost three last week." Willie and I looked at one another, and we were shaken. The full fighter squadron complement of pilots was twenty-two, and there were at that time less than fifteen of us including Willie and myself, so the law of averages did not make life look too promising for us. At the time, the squadron was mainly employed in dive-bombing heavily defended targets, such as bridges and railway marshalling yards, and low-level strafing of transport columns. There had been many casualties.

The heavy losses in the squadron made the pilots spend their leisure time at a feverish pace. Everything took on an air of "Let's take it while we are still around to enjoy it." We had many parties in the cellar with an Italian band to provide the music, stylishly attired in party clothing with red coats and black trousers. They usually started with ingratiating smiles and beaming countenances, which usually changed to stares of puzzlement and sheepish smiles when the pilots started acting wildly.

My first operation after joining the squadron was to attack the Casarsa rail junction in the northern plain of Italy. It was a mad scramble for me to try to keep up with the veterans, who coped easily with the pattern of taking off bunched closely, then forming into tight line-astern formations before moving into their finger formations of four aircraft per flight—twelve aircraft altogether when in full squadron strength.

After getting airborne, we started our long climb and made our way up the coast of Italy toward Casarsa staying over the Adriatic to avoid the German anti-aircraft batteries. When we got to the bend in the coastline after Venice, we edged in to fly over land as we prepared ourselves for the attack.

As we crossed the coast at 9,000 feet, the blasts of anti-aircraft fire got closer as the gunners found their range and height. The leader started weaving and flying an erratic course with the rest of the squadron following suit. In a moment, there was a sudden change from our neat straight-

and-level formation flying to a wild procession of aircraft acting like flies, up and down to the left and right. I had difficulty keeping my place behind my lead aircraft while taking care not to collide with the other weaving and twisting fighters near me.

When we approached the target area and the leader signaled us to form into stepped echelon, formation order returned to the gaggle of heavily loaded airplanes. I concentrated on keeping my position among the other Kittyhawks and tried not to let the shouting in my earphones distract my attention.

As we approached the target, the shell bursts came closer. When the leader rolled over onto his back and entered his dive, I followed him closely. The rail tracks converging on the marshalling yard appeared directly below the nose of my aircraft. The scream of the slipstream got louder, and my Kitty was buffeted from side to side.

I edged my gun sight up toward the center of the marshalling yard, and then pressed the red bomb-release button. I felt the release of the weight of my 1,000-pound bomb and immediately pulled back hard on the stick. As I zoomed upward and to the side, the shells continued bursting nearby.

Each of us searched for the rendezvous point where we had to fit into the circular line-astern pattern. The sky was full of our aircraft, and for me, on my first raid, it was particularly confusing. I had to identify the planes of my own squadron. After careening around among the many fighters in the area, I managed to locate my companions and joined the closely bunched group of twelve aircraft. As soon as we were settled, the mission leader signaled to head home.

As we began our return flight I saw that all positions in the formation were filled and no one was missing. I began to relax, knowing that I had been through the baptism of fire on my first operational mission. Everything happened so quickly, but I was sure that the next mission would be easier. I had a feeling of satisfaction at knowing that I had completed my first operational mission and that I had overcome fear.

During my second mission, to dive-bomb a heavily defended target near Padua, I had a mortifying experience. I didn't realize I had left my radio transmitter in the transmit mode, and every word and curse that I uttered was heard by the entire force, preventing radio communication between any of the other aircraft. I am not the only pilot who talks to himself when on a raid, cursing the anti-aircraft fire, the leader of the formation, and anything else. Imagine my dismay when I realized that every word I had said was heard by everyone in the air on that frequency. After landing the leader, a shy young Englishman innocently asked me why I had cursed him. I hastened to explain that it was nothing personal and that it was only my way of releasing tension during the mission.

KADIMAH!

We had attacked some tough targets, but the worst was Padua. It was a target that always worried us when it was planned, because the city and its immediate environs contained a bridge and marshalling yard complex. This transport nexus seemed to be of special importance to the Germans and was heavily defended by anti-aircraft guns of all calibers. It was such a hot spot that we took care not to fly near it when on the way to other targets.

Raids were often led by the squadron commander, though important targets were sometimes led by the wing commander. Sometimes, one of the more experienced pilots, usually one nearing the end of his tour of operations, acted as leader. Often, it was not a pilot of officer rank, and I remember one raid by all six squadrons of our wing involving more than seventy aircraft that was superbly led by a sergeant pilot near the end of his tour.

When another raid on Padua was announced by the squadron intelligence officer, a collective groan rose from the pilots. The pilot selected to lead the three squadrons this time was a Canadian, who had returned from a mission not long before with one of his wings riddled with bullet holes. His name was Jim Duval. Like others near the end of their tour, he had lost weight from the strain of waiting for his tour to end. Superstitiously, we believed the chances of getting hit were higher during the last few raids of our tours.

The raid was in the late morning. The sun was shining through the haze as we approached the target. Everything looked peaceful and quiet, only a little smoke from the industrial area and no traffic on the roads. Within minutes we saw the white puffs of the Bofors anti-aircraft guns, directed at 260 Squadron, the first of our wing to attack the target. I saw Jim wheel over onto his back as he went into the dive. We followed him down but soon realized he was not pulling out of his dive.

Because he was senior to me and leading the mission, I hesitated; before I could even shout to him on my radio he dived right into the ground. All that was left was a small cloud of dust. There was no evidence of a bomb burst around him, but a pillar of smoke to one side was proof that he had allowed his bomb to skid away from its intended trajectory. A highly experienced dive-bomber pilot, he must have been hit during the dive. We formed up around his number two at the rendezvous point in the usual way after the raid and made our way sadly back to base.

We had taken off from our strip near the village of Cervia, where we had moved from Fano. It is a seaside resort farther north up the Adriatic coast and not far from Ravenna. In Cervia we operated from another metal strip in sand dunes near the sea, and our wing this time was the sole occupant of the narrow strip. The juxtaposition of the metal strip in the sand dunes and the peaceful beachfront was a poignant contrast. Peace and war and destruction living side by side. I had the same feeling whenever an environment of peace and normality at the base was followed by short operational missions that transport one into battle and back, unlike foot soldiers, in a matter of hours or even minutes.

One afternoon in February 1945, after returning from bombing and strafing an area around a bridge in the north, which was particularly heavily defended by anti-aircraft guns, Willie and I sat down with a glass of wine. (One of our Kittyhawks flew regularly to Sicily to bring back wine in two drop tanks, cooled on the way by flying back at 20,000 feet. We made sure that this aircraft was always at the ready whatever the exigencies of the military situation.)

We were taking a sip of the sweet marsala wine when we were interrupted by the sound of firing from the direction of the coast. We walked down to the beach where infantrymen were practicing with anti-tank guns. They did not look like British troops, though they were dressed in British army battledress. They were speaking in a foreign language.

A tall blond officer shouted something to his men. The word he used was "Kadimah." At that time I knew no Hebrew beyond the little that I had learned for my Bar Mitzvah some six years before, but I knew some other words from my time in the Habonim youth movement and recognized the word, which meant "forward."

Strong emotions ran through me when I realized that Jewish soldiers from Palestine were fighting here beside me. As soon as the exercise ended, I approached the officer and introduced myself saying, "I heard you speaking Hebrew and understand that you are from Palestine." He answered, "Yes, we are in the Jewish Brigade. What are you?" I replied, "I am a South African from a Zionist family with connections in Palestine and the Yishuv."

We struck up an immediate bond, and when I visited their officers' mess that night, we talked about the war and our respective roles. They were part of the second battalion of the Jewish Brigade and were carrying out their final training before moving up to the front in Alfonsine not far ahead of us. Events prevented me from establishing contact again, but I heard much later in Israel that the same officer,

Danny Cornfeld, was again an officer, this time in the Israeli forces during the War of Independence. Neither of us could have guessed that we would be fighting together in the same armed force in Israel in a little more than two years.

Those of us on duty would sit around waiting for the signal to take off. We were galvanized into action when we heard the gaggle horn, an English hunting horn connected to the exhaust of a truck. When the engine was started it gave out a strident blast, enough to warn if any Germans were within five kilometers of us. We would then race to the field in our own truck, which was bizarrely equipped with a beautiful antique armchair upholstered in yellow silk. There were also other odd pieces of furniture "lifted" from houses in the area.

Not long afterward, I flew my mission to Venice and ended up in the sea.

CHAPTER FOUR

Zion

LONDON AND FLYING STEEPLE CHASE

AFTER having had some exposure to Europe during my service, I felt that I needed to move on from South Africa to try my chances in the outside world. I decided to begin my studies at the London School of Economics.

London, despite its gaping war wounds, still maintained its proud image. The Londoners wore their threadbare and faded clothes with pride. At the London School of Economics (L.S.E.) the environment wasn't like the university I attended in Johannesburg. It is on Houghton Street on a city block, with virtually no campus life as I knew it. The students came in the morning for lectures and went home in the evening. There were occasional functions, usually political meetings with a strong bent toward the left.

L.S.E. seethed with political turmoil and was a center of socialist intellectualism in Europe. The makeup of the political organizations at the university showed this. There were about a thousand members of the Soc-Soc or Socialist Society and less than a hundred members of the Conservative Society. Anything with a tinge of the right wing or belief in free enterprise was decried as fascist. Not being a political animal, I joined the marginal student Zionist society.

In the first winter, I went to Swedish Lapland for a skiing holiday. Having been neutral during the war, Sweden's shops had all the things not seen for years in England, and I was amazed at the luxury everywhere. The peacetime tempo and atmosphere and the absence of the shortages, which I had encountered in postwar England, were striking. While at the ski resort, I met a Swedish girl, and when we returned to Stockholm, she invited me to her parents' home. On the living room piano, there were many family photographs. Almost without exception the men in the photographs were in Swedish military uniform. Katerina explained that her uncle was one of the king's brothers. Two years later I was to meet him in Israel as Count Folke Bernadotte, head of the United Nations's mission in the Middle East. Shortly after his arrival, he was assassinated in Israel by the Stern Group.

Living in London was very stimulating, and though there was much to see and do, I started flying again. I discovered that as a former pilot in an RAF squadron, I could hire small aircraft at subsidized rates. I began to fly to France and Switzerland on weekends and on vacations from the university.

The Palestine Club was not far from Piccadilly Circus. One Sunday evening I went to the club and met up with a few Palestinian Jews. One of them was a tall gangly fellow with blue eyes and a mischievous look. We soon discovered that we were the same age and had both been fighter pilots in the RAF during the war. He was Ezer Weizman, nephew of Chaim Weizmann. Ezer was studying aeronautical engineering at a polytechnic in London. We struck up a close friendship based on our common flying interests and our total commitment to Zionism.

I took Ezer with me on flights when I rented aircraft from the RAF flying club at Panshangar near Hatfield. Some of the flights were in a tiny Moth Minor with two open cockpits in tandem and others in an Auster Autocrat. I paid the princely sum of four pounds a day plus fuel and insurance and made several trips to France and Switzerland. One such flight was memorable and is an example of how not to do things.

I had planned to go to Arosa in Switzerland for a skiing holiday with a girlfriend and asked Ezer to come with me to fly the aircraft back to England while I stayed on. We flew to Lympne near the Channel coast to pass through customs and immigration formalities. The weather was bad, and the airlines were all grounded. But I pressed on, hoping that if we ran into difficulties we could either return or land somewhere. Shortly after takeoff, we ran into clouds and couldn't see the ground. Neither of us had instrument ratings and precious little instrument time, and we soon got into difficulties. The cloud was dense and dark, indicating that we were flying into a cumulonimbus storm cloud, the scourge of all pilots.

Immediately after we entered the cloud, turbulence began to throw us around the sky like a shuttlecock. Driving rain interspersed with sheets of hail pounded on the thin windows of the tiny craft as we bounced, ducked, and dived. Mighty updrafts of air pressed us violently against our seats as we were lifted hundreds of feet at a time, followed by sickening plunges. I had difficulty controlling the aircraft as the airspeed increased at an alarming rate while I put the Auster into a climb, dumbfounding me completely. The more I pulled back on the stick to climb to reduce speed, the more the speed built up. The altimeter showed we were losing height at a terrifying rate.

Fortunately, we broke out of the cloud at 4,000 feet and were shaken to find that we were in a near-vertical dive. With hindsight, of course, it is simple to understand what happened. We had gotten into a spiral dive without realizing it, and I was tightening the spiral by pulling back on the stick. If we had had more instrument time and training, usually a low priority for fighter pilots, we would have known what was happening and could have solved the problem by first leveling our wings and then pulling the stick back to reduce the speed. It is difficult to describe the magnitude of the disorientation when flying in clouds without using instruments.

Shaken and embarrassed by our poor airmanship, we continued across the Channel en route to Lille in northern France to refuel. While over the middle of the Channel, the turbulence became so severe that the compass deviation card jumped out of its slot on to the floor. We picked up heavy icing, and with low clouds and near-zero visibility, we had difficulty finding Lille. When we eventually reached it and landed, we found that the field was closed to air traffic and the main runway was barely visible. After all we had been through, there was no fuel available.

On the next leg, we spotted an airfield, and while circling noted a flag flying above the control tower. Neither of us recognized it. After landing we found that it was the Belgian flag, and the field was a military base at Courtrai. The air force men there were obliging, causing us no trouble for landing without permission. At that time shortly after World War II, there were very few small private airplanes flying from country to country, and we were invariably received with a mixture of curiosity and amusement. The military field had no fuel suitable for our aircraft and we left immediately.

At this time we were short of fuel and night was coming on; I was worried that we would soon be running out of daylight. We were without night flying equipment and instruments so I decided to continue as quickly as possible to Brussels. By the time we arrived there, it was almost dark. Shortly after landing, while taxiing to the dispersal area, we ran out of fuel and the engine stopped. That proved how extremely foolhardy we were in flying into the night without instruments or fuel.

I found the Shell agent and after refueling the Auster he obligingly smuggled us out of the airport in his van, for we were without visas. The following morning we left for Basle in Switzerland. The weather was still bad, but eventually we found our way. As we approached the field, I turned as usual into a left-hand circuit. However, seeing a large cloud reaching down to the ground close on the side of the field near the airport, I decided to do a right-hand circuit and landed. There was no air traffic in the area. At the field there was only a skeleton staff, who were surprised to see a light plane flying when all large aircraft were grounded because of the weather. When we had settled down, I asked them whether they knew the reason for the cloud almost on the field and extending right down to the deck. They said, "Don't you know that cloud covers a mountain? This field has a mandatory right-hand pattern." We must have used up about three lives on that reckless flight.

A new problem arose. I did not need a Swiss visa because of my South African passport, but Ezer was in trouble with his Palestinian passport and no visa. We explored every possibility and finally Ezer exclaimed, "My Uncle Chaim is here at the Zionist Congress! Let's try and get his help." After inquiries, he telephoned Chaim Weizmann at the Drei Könige Hotel, the venue for the Zionist Congress, and he arranged entry for his nephew into Switzerland. We arrived at the hotel in our flying togs, looking scruffy and quite unlike the elegantly attired delegates at the congress.

Chaim Weizmann was kind to us, and I spent some time chatting with him. He seemed uneasy and asked me while pointing to delegates who were sitting at a nearby table, "Are they some of ours?" I did not understand who he was referring to, but it was later explained to me that he meant the Revisionist delegates who were the main opposition party to the mainstream Zionists. I heard later that as he advanced in years he became paranoid about the Revisionist opposition and in particular about their leader Menachem Begin.

After one night I took the train to Arosa and left Ezer to

fly the Auster back to England. On the way back, he got lost and after landing in a field to ask directions, he damaged a wing when he struck a fence during takeoff. He patched it up with adhesive tape and eventually got back to Panshangar in England.

SAM BENNET

My first confrontation with the horrors of the Holocaust came when I went to the cinema in 1945 in London. Customary at that time, a long newsreel was shown before the main film. It started with some mundane news about the end of the war in Europe, and then without warning, a film appeared about the Nazi death camps. The pictures of the skeletal Jewish prisoners, the gas chambers, and the crematoria threw my mind into turmoil, and I walked the streets of London in a daze.

Deeply disturbed and feeling more Jewish than I had ever felt before, I tried to learn more about the Holocaust. I sought out survivors of the death camps to hear firsthand accounts of the atrocities. It was hard to learn many of the details, for understandably, the survivors were reluctant to recount their experiences. But by late 1945, information about the Holocaust was beginning to appear, and I delved deeply into the history of those years.

Initially, my search was to find out how millions of my race and religion had gone to the gas chambers, virtually without resistance. It took me a long time to understand the situation of the victims and the environment in which they were living at the time. I began to understand how the cold, starving Jews were overwhelmed by the meetings with the apparently invincible members of the German master race.

I was shattered by the evidence of the cold, inhuman machinery of death, which was tacitly accepted in Europe, even by those who resisted the German armed forces. I will never understand how the rest of the world stood by and did virtually nothing to stop the mass murder of our people. It is common knowledge that this huge operation was known to the intelligence forces of the Allies early in the war. When I learned that the Allies bombed a synthetic rubber plant five kilometers from the ovens of Auschwitz, I became convinced that there could be no justification for the Allies not having at least bombed the gas chambers and ovens. The casualties that might have been caused to the inmates who were in any case destined to be gassed would have been a fraction of the total numbers of deaths. Even bombing the railway lines leading to the death camps might have saved many innocent people, and the announcement of these raids and their purpose might have stopped the seeming indifference by the Allies to what was happening.

I have no doubt that we Jewish pilots would have succeeded for we had sufficient fuel to reach Poland, and our bombing was accurate enough. Had the intelligence services of the Allies told us about the monstrous death factories, we could have substantially reduced the scale of the tragedy.

Having been brought up in a civilized society without once having encountered organized cruelty or even overt anti-Semitism, I was traumatized by what I saw and heard.

My naive trust in the innate goodness of humanity evaporated, and the world changed for me. Even more alarming, my belief in God was deeply shaken. If God is all-powerful, how could he have allowed the slaughter of more than a million and a half Jewish children?

The horrors of the Holocaust were a turning point for me. From that time on, the course of my life changed completely and the Holocaust became the leitmotif of my life. Instead of being a run-of the-mill student who would have completed his studies and returned to his hometown and to the business and the protection of his family, I chose a completely different course. I had known in a general way that the Nazis were persecuting my people, and I had believed that there was some maltreatment. I never imagined the scope of the horror, however, that went on night and day for four years in an attempt to rid the world of anyone with Jewish blood. I was driven by an intense desire to exact revenge. It did not take me long to realize that there was no way for me to do so, years after the abominations, and that I must instead find some means for positive action on behalf of the Jews.

My studies in the second year at university became trivial, irrelevant. I contacted the United Nations Relief and Rehabilitation Association (UNRRA) and applied to go to the Continent to assist the so ineptly labeled "Displaced Persons," who were the pitifully few survivors of the death camps. Despite my efforts, I couldn't find any meaningful way in which to participate in their work.

In a state of utmost desperation, I sought a way to react to the terrible happenings. It quickly became clear that the only course left was Zionism, to establish an independent state, a haven and homeland for the survivors of the camps and the last refuge in this world from animosity for Jews anywhere. The realization of the 2,000-year-old dream of the return to our own country could be the only fitting epitaph for our slaughtered people. I prepared myself for the struggle to create an independent Jewish homeland in Palestine.

In the mood of despair in which I found myself in 1946, I approached in London an old friend of the family from Johannesburg, Samuel Katz. He was a slim, bespectacled man who bore a strong resemblance to his mentor in the Revisionist movement of Zionism, Ze'ev Jabotinsky. He was an intellectual and an authority on Jewish history and customs, particularly the history of political Zionism.

Though creating the impression of a quiet, studious intellectual, he had always been a firebrand Zionist member of the Revisionist party. When the time came for overt action, he became an active member of the Irgun Zvai Leumi (National Military Organization), the military arm of the party. He detested what he called the liberal attitude of the mainstream parties in Palestine such as the Mapai Labour Movement. He disliked Chaim Weizmann, referring to his approach as "another cow and another dunam" policy, meaning the gradual, peaceful, and orderly progress toward setting up an independent state. In view of what happened to the Jewish communities in the Holocaust, few would dispute the Irgun's urgent activist policy of fighting with all means to ensure the immediate establishment of an independent state that would open its borders to Jews everywhere.

Far away in sunny and peaceful South Africa, in more or less complete ignorance of what was happening to our brethren under the Nazis, my family and I had considered the Revisionists to be a committed but violent group, and I did not find enough common ground to support them.

At the time, the British and society in general considered the Irgun Zvai Leumi as a dangerous terrorist organization. Despite my inner conflict and knowing that by joining the Irgun in an active role I would be crossing the line from the background in which I had been raised, I made a firm decision to espouse unreservedly by any means, however violent, the aim of founding an independent state that would shelter the remnants of the Jewish population of Europe. Though I realized this step might cost me dearly during the bitter struggle ahead, this about-face in my life was essential for my own peace of mind.

With great secrecy, Katz introduced me to one of the Irgun activists in London. Having all my life been an Anglophile, educated for five years at a very British public school in Natal and having served as an officer in an RAF fighter squadron, I was torn between my allegiance to Britain and the Commonwealth. I took sides in what would clearly be a bitter struggle against Britain to achieve our goal. I joined the Irgun in England as an active member of the organization, knowing full well that this move would place me in direct conflict with the British government and possibly also the country of my birth. South Africa was at that time still a part of the British Commonwealth.

Shortly after joining the Irgun, I was sent to Paris for training in underground tactics. My first meeting in Paris with the commanders of the Irgun was at the Lutetia Hotel on Boulevard Raspail, headquarters of the Irgun in Europe. Katz's familiarity with the members whom I met reassured me somewhat after the tales that appeared daily in the British press about the bloodthirsty terrorists who comprised the Irgun fighters. Shortly after arriving in Paris, I was given a nom de guerre to be used in our Irgun activities. I became "Samuel Bennet."

"Benjamin" was the code name of the commander of Irgun Europe, and I discovered his real identity only many years later, Eliahu Lankin. He was unassuming, of medium height, and his spectacles gave him a studious air. He was soft-spoken, cultured, and gentle, the last person one would suspect of being a terrorist. Only the fact that in the middle of the European winter he was deeply sunburned gave a clue to his having escaped shortly before from Eritrea, where he had been deported by the British Mandate authorities in Palestine. The British often deported Palestinian Jews they suspected of being Irgun terrorists.

Benjamin had escaped from Eritrea and spent days under the false floor of a bus traveling across Africa to Europe. In both Hebrew and English, he had a strong Russian accent. Years before he had escaped from Russian pogroms to Manchuria with his parents. Having been at school in Harbin, Manchuria, he spoke passably good Chinese and was for me a source of curiosity and pride in Chinese restaurants in Paris.

He was assisted by a group of Jews from Palestine and eastern Europe. A few of them bore the blue numbers the Nazis had tattooed on the arms of all Jews who had been incarcerated in the death camps. They all had only one overwhelming aim: the creation of a Jewish homeland. Some of my Irgun compatriots were the only survivors of families murdered in the Holocaust and bore their own guilt for not having done anything to help.

There were also a few Americans. One of the women was Ziporah, who acted as secretary and organized train and plane tickets. All of us were motivated by the principle of getting rid of the British rulers of our future homeland as soon as possible. The only occasion on which I had a feeling of distaste was when one, an American called Rifkind, spoke of his admiration for the Hollywood screenwriter Ben Hecht's public declaration that "he had a holiday in his heart" every time he heard that a British soldier was killed in Palestine.

The French government conformed to its traditional attitude toward political refugees and its displeasure at the ousting of French influence by the British in the Middle East. The French were not only tolerant of the Irgun contingent but, when pressured by the British government to undertake action against the Irgun members in Paris, gave timely warnings to allow the hurried evacuation of a hotel and a move to another location.

In Palestine considerable friction existed among the three underground groups. Sometimes the enmity boiled over into bitter struggles between the mainstream Haganah, the military arm of the more moderate labor-led factions, and the more extreme Irgun and Stern organizations. Among those of our group who had not been through the hell of the Nazi death camps were some Jewish Palestinians, who

had from their earliest youth been members of the ultra-
nationalist Revisionists and had been in conflict with the
Haganah. One of the Jewish Palestinians in Paris with the
Irgun was Eli Tavin, who maintained that he had been captured and tied to a bed for ten days by the Haganah after
taking part in the Irgun bombing of the British embassy in
Rome.

We were taught how to make primitive bombs and time-
delay fuses using a small acid container, which, after breaking, let the acid gradually penetrate a piece of camera film,
detonating the explosive. One target was the commander of
the British forces in Palestine, Gen. Evelyn Barker. He had
brutally turned back the immigrant ships carrying concentration camp survivors seeking refuge and had confirmed
death warrants to execute a number of Irgun fighters. The
Irgun had also warned him that floggings, which were carried out by the British, and death sentences would incur
like treatment for the occupying British administration. In
addition, Barker had published an official order of the day
to his troops in Palestine, "putting all Jewish businesses and
private houses out of bounds . . . to punish the Jews in the
manner which this race dislikes most by hitting them in
their pockets." This statement in particular helped to make
him a target of the Irgun.

The British Irgun members could act only in a support-
ing role, for none had any experience in handling delayed-
action bombs. Discussions were held in Paris about how to
get an experienced member from the Palestine Irgun into
England for this purpose. We knew the British authorities

were keeping a close watch on all ports and airfields, aware of the Irgun intention to bring men into the United Kingdom to retaliate for what was being done by British troops and the Palestine police. It seemed an impossible mission to get anyone into the country; as a last resort, I volunteered to smuggle someone in by air. My suggestion was accepted and I returned to London.

Back in London I contacted my friend Ezer and told him of having joined the Irgun, and I explained my intention to start operations by smuggling someone into England. He, too, was frustrated by his inability to do anything. I requested his help and he readily agreed to join the Irgun. I moved from Kensington to digs in his building so that we could prepare for the mission from there. Because of his Palestinian passport, I knew it would be unwise for him to play anything more than a low-profile role. His job would be to take the bomb expert away from the landing area if I succeeded in getting him into England. Ezer's decision to join the Irgun eventually led to his making an outstanding political career with the Likud party, which had its antecedents in the Irgun. When the Likud came to power, Ezer became the Defense Minister. In 1993 he became president of Israel as, of course, was his uncle Chaim Weizmann before him.

I had misgivings about what we intended to accomplish in England. It is hard to project oneself back so long ago in time to examine the morality of one's intentions and actions. For us it was war with no holds barred. I was a Jew first, and as such, for me, the end justified the means.

YOEL

Irgun headquarters in Paris found a most suitable person to organize the British operation, a young man from Palestine named Yoel, who had served in the British army during the war and spoke passable English with a Welsh accent, which he acquired when serving in a Welsh regiment during World War II. He was a quiet young man, totally devoted to the Irgun and its cause. With his pale complexion, I was sure he would pass for an Englishman if questioned by the police.

In preparation for the coming operation, I bought from the Auster company a new three-seat aircraft with a high wing and a 100-horsepower engine. British registration was G-AIZV, and it appeared to be my private aircraft. It was noisy in the cabin and underpowered, but I felt it would do the job. To become familiar with its flying characteristics and, at the same time, to possibly throw Scotland Yard off the scent, I made two innocent flights to Paris and one to Barcelona.

After a search from the ground and from the air, I chose a small field, part of a farm near Canterbury. The field was in an isolated farming area, and small, but with the advantage of being ringed with trees, although they were high enough to present a danger during takeoff and landing. A significant plus was that the field was under the flight path for light aircraft flying between Paris and London.

After practicing short landings and takeoffs in the Auster, I flew to Paris. I chose a grass airfield near the city as the pick-up point for my unofficial passenger. Ezer was in England before I went to Paris, and I arranged that he hire a car and take with him a female sympathizer named Deborah. They were to cruise slowly around the landing field in England at the appointed time as though they were a young couple looking for a quiet spot. If I succeeded in my mission to fly Yoel into England, Ezer was to pick him up and drive him to our digs in London while I took off immediately for my official destination at Croydon.

On the day of the mission, the weather was bright and promising, and from the window of my room in the little Hotel Royal on Boulevard Raspail, I scanned the sky for clouds. The feeling of exhilaration for the mission I had to accomplish was tempered with some foreboding. Having served as an officer in His Majesty's Royal Air Force only a short two years before, I imagined my fate if I were caught smuggling an Irgun terrorist into England.

After a French breakfast of hot croissants and bitter coffee, I paid my bill. I spent some minutes examining the parked cars and passing traffic. When I was satisfied that there seemed to be no representatives of British Intelligence in the area, I bought a *Daily Mail* printed in Paris. I smiled at the headline: Irgun Terrorists Trying to Enter England All Ports and Airfields Guarded. I took a taxi to the light-aircraft field at Toussus le Noble and kept the copy of the *Daily Mail* to carry in the aircraft with me.

The Auster was parked with its chocks on the grass. The immigration and customs officials were as usual perfunctory in their examination, and I smiled when one of them said, "*Le jour est jolie.* Don't lose your way."

I submitted a flight plan direct to Croydon at a height of

4,000 feet with a flight time of two hours and fifty minutes. I had added about twenty minutes to cover the unofficial detours. The forecast was for good visibility with about one-third of the sky overcast with broken clouds at 3,000 feet. That looked good to me, affording cover for my straying from the flight path to England. I spent some time poring over the maps to satisfy myself that I could stray from my flight path after takeoff and again after crossing the English Channel without inviting too many questions from the French and British air traffic control authorities.

After takeoff from Toussus le Noble, I headed for the airfield where I intended to collect Yoel. Apart from two gliders circling nearby, there was no air traffic in the area. Time was important because I had to keep as closely as possible to the flight plan. I lost height rapidly in a steep dive and landed close to the clump of trees on one side of the field. A car was parked nearby.

I taxied fast to the trees and toward the group of five men and women, whom I had arranged would sidle up to look at the aircraft. I kept the engine running, and Yoel leapt into the plane while the rest retreated to the trees, bunched fairly close together so that nobody would notice that whereas five had come to the aircraft only four had retired to the trees. I took off quickly and climbed to cruising altitude in a northwesterly direction.

I had met Yoel only once before our flight but remembered him as an earnest young man not in the habit of wasting his breath in idle talk. Though we scarcely exchanged a word during the entire flight, I am sure that Yoel felt the bond between us.

When I saw the coast ahead and the English Channel, I opened the throttle, climbed to 12,000 feet, and eased back to a more-lean mixture. After my experience in the cold Adriatic off Venice two years before, I always took care when crossing the Channel to climb high enough to ensure that in case of failure of the single engine I would be able to glide either to England or to France. We got to 12,000 feet just before reaching mid-Channel, and I began to glide using short bursts of engine on the way down to prevent carburetor icing.

When the white cliffs of Dover appeared ahead, I lost height rapidly and began searching for the field near Canterbury. The tarred road appeared to the north of the field, and I followed it until I was sure of my target. I had made it exactly on time and could see a vehicle, presumably Ezer's, at the northern border of the field just beyond the low stone wall marking the edge of the property.

I flew one circuit of the field to verify there were no busybodies in the area and made a steep approach with plenty of power and a nose-up attitude to ensure a minimal landing run. Over the high trees almost at stalling speed, I made a hard landing. Before the aircraft had stopped its run toward the trees and the waiting car, I shouted to Yoel to jump out and run.

As soon as I saw him climb over the wall and into the waiting car, I swung the Auster around and took off hurriedly. Thirty minutes later, I landed at Croydon and taxied to the tower. Though my heart was pounding from excitement, I tried to walk as nonchalantly as I could toward the police and the customs sheds.

Though I had made the two detours in quick time, arriving only shortly after the time I had entered in my flight plan, the officials must have been tipped off, for as soon as I entered their office I sensed something was wrong. Their polite but thorough questioning confirmed my suspicions. I had by then made a number of flights to the Continent to put them off the scent, and only perfunctory questions had been posed to me by the customs and immigration officers in the past.

This time, though, they obviously were suspicious. They subjected me to a barrage of questions about what I had been doing in Paris, why I had flown there, and so on. I thought I fielded their questions satisfactorily but subsequent events proved they did suspect me of something. In the meantime, I was sure that Ezer and Yoel were well on their way to London.

After passing through the checks and completing the formalities connected with the aircraft, I made for my quarters in Bayswater, where I had moved to be with Ezer. By the time I arrived, Ezer and Yoel were already there. We were soon joined by Paul, a suave Irgun sympathizer who spoke English and French perfectly.

After settling down we began the search for General Barker. Our Irgun contact in London owned a large, black Hudson Terraplane car. We covered hundreds of miles in our search, struck up a friendship with the local publican in the area of his family home, and spent many hours in the bar, but had no success. We also scouted around one of the military camps reputed to have been his base unit, but he seemed to have disappeared into thin air. We had no backup intelligence force and had to rely on ourselves for everything: the search for Barker, preparation of the mission, and everything else. In retrospect, it is clear that we had not done enough preparatory work before the operation.

During the hunt for General Barker, and while I was in my room, the housekeeper of our building in Kensington Gardens Square whispered to me in a confidential tone, "The coppers are here asking for you." She could have had no idea of what we were up to as we had always acted like two students attending lectures at the university. She must have sensed they were police.

I felt vulnerable because they wanted to question me in my room, which was full of incriminating printed material from Palestine, and the walls were covered with maps of England, France, and Belgium. They seemed to know a lot about me and asked if I had friends in Paris. They were quite pleasant, questioning me politely without threatening. The man in charge was an Inspector Dyer, and though he acted correctly throughout the questioning, he was obviously suspicious. I later learned that Dyer was in charge of the Palestine desk.

The next move came from the Civil Aviation authorities. I was called to appear before them. They cancelled my flying license without explanation.

In the end, the operation failed because we couldn't find General Barker, and I left for Johannesburg. Ezer and Yoel were told that they were not welcome in the United Kingdom and had to leave. When I was about to board the flight from London to Lisbon to catch the Pan American flight to

Johannesburg, there was consultation and argument among the immigration officials at the airfield. I was sure they were arguing about whether to let me leave.

When I arrived in Johannesburg with forty-four other passengers, I was called to the passport control officer before any of the other passengers. The man in charge turned to me and in an Afrikaans accent asked me, "Man, what have you been doing? The police all over the world are inquiring about you. Even if you had landed in Hong Kong, the British would be waiting for you!" His strong accent left no doubt in my mind about his sympathies. He was certainly not pro-British. Whatever the reason, I was not detained and went home to my anxious parents.

NEWCOMER

The struggle for a national home in Palestine became the focus of world Jewry and offers of support poured in from Jewish centers the world over. After Britain prevented refugees who had managed to survive the Holocaust from finding a haven in Palestine, it was decided that Jewish nationhood and independence had to be achieved whatever the cost. After years of activity and lobbying on the part of Jewish organizations and the unrest as a result of the attacks by the Irgun in Palestine and abroad, the United Nations Organization in November 1947 voted and decreed that Palestine was to be partitioned into two states, one Jewish and one Arab. The vote had the support of the Soviet Union and the United States, while Britain abstained. The decision was a cause of rejoicing for all Jews and disappointment and opposition for the Arabs of Palestine. The British government decided that the end of the mandate was to be on 15 May 1948 and that Britain would evacuate Palestine by that date. War between Arabs and Jews was inevitable in Palestine.

For many months before the UN resolution on partition, the opposing forces had begun organizing. The Jews had some 20,000 Haganah fighters and 3,000 Palmach (shock troops), which were trained mainly in commando tactics and night fighting. The Palmach had its origin during World War II when it was partly financed by the British. After the danger of a German invasion of Palestine passed, it went underground because of the British policy of banning arms for Jews.

The Palmach units moved to kibbutzim and worked part time while continuing their military exercises. No wages were paid, and this elite unit became the training ground for leading generals of the future Israeli army: Moshe Dayan, Yitzhak Rabin, Yitzhak Sadeh, and Yigael Alon. The force was finally disbanded and absorbed into the official Israeli army in November 1948 during the War of Independence. The Irgun's much smaller groups were based in the cities with the main thrust of their activities directed against British military forces in Palestine and abroad. Facing them were 10,000 soldiers of the Arab Legion (which used British officers), with its armor and artillery financed and supported by Britain. There were many thousands of trained Arab irregulars. At that time, but still in the background, were tens of thousands of men in the standing armies of

Egypt, Syria, Lebanon, Iraq, and Saudi Arabia who were soon to be committed to the forthcoming battle. All these armies were equipped with the arms of a regular national army, and many of them were stationed on the borders of Palestine well before the end of the mandate.

As soon as the partition was announced, I booked a seat on the first available aircraft from Johannesburg to Tel Aviv in the hope of being able to consummate the dream Ezer and I had talked about in London, namely, the creation of an air force, which would play a key role in the establishment of an independent Jewish state in Palestine.

The long flight from Johannesburg to Palestine took three days with nine refueling stops en route. It was in a four-engine Lancaster bomber converted to carry fourteen passengers in relative comfort despite the lack of pressurization. I had cabled Ezer that I was coming, and when we landed at Lydda Airport, a flight controller gave me a message from Ezer, inviting me to Haifa to stay with his family. The controller was Yariv Sheinbaum, a former RAF pilot, who later flew a Norseman bombing Arab troops near Beit Mahsir, scene of fierce battles between Arab irregulars and the Palmach. Neither of us could have imagined that within a few months of our first meeting we would be in the air attacking the same target from different aircraft, nor that Yariv would not return from that mission.

As Ezer was busy in Tel Aviv at that time, I was to go to Haifa to stay with his parents, and they received me warmly. They lived in a pleasant stone house on Melchett Street, and I immediately sensed the informality that still pervades life in Israel today when Ezer's father slouched into my bedroom wearing slippers and carrying a glass of black tea. I had met Ezer's father when he came to London in 1947, and it helped me to be with someone familiar when I first arrived in a country with an environment so different from my own background.

My first mission in Haifa was to contact Abraham Rutenberg, the main shareholder in the electric companies in Palestine. Rutenberg had British partners in the power stations, and before World War II, they had invested in a small airline, which flew from Haifa to Beirut. During the war the company had ceased operations, and the erstwhile partners in the flying venture were interested in recouping their investment by resuscitating the airline destined to be called Palestine Airways. I had discussed the project with South African businessmen, who were prepared to assist in financing the airline. In Haifa we were joined for discussions by the manager of a large British nonscheduled airline interested in taking part in the project. However, my own plans for the airline came to nothing when I joined the fledgling air arm of the Haganah two days after I arrived in the country in December 1947.

FROM IRGUN TO THE HAGANAH

The Haganah general staff gave its tiny air arm the name *Sherut Avir,* which means "air service." The headquarters were on Montefiore Street in Tel Aviv under the name "General Council of Jewish Aviation." Besides a few pilots, there was one mechanic at the airfield of Sde Dov in Tel

Aviv, and eight or nine others dealing with engineering, operations, and supply matters, some former RAF members and some stalwarts of the Histadrut (General Trade Union).

Though the die was already cast for me after joining the air service of the Haganah, I was not entirely at peace with my decision to leave the Irgun's ranks. I wanted to discuss my position with Menachem Begin, the commander of the still-separate Irgun. In the years during which the Irgun carried out attacks against the British in Palestine and in Europe, Begin, the underground "terrorist leader," had been the scourge of the government of Great Britain. Though he was the commander of the Irgun when I was in Paris, I had not met him before. As the most hunted man by the British authorities in Palestine with hanging his fate if ever caught, it was not an easy task to arrange a meeting. His whereabouts were a secret even to those working closely with him. He was reputed to move daily from hideout to hideout. Being hunted by the British was for him nothing new because he had been imprisoned by the Soviets and sentenced to eight years hard labor in the Arctic Circle.

The schism between the Haganah and the Irgun was so deep that it was impossible to be a member of one force while even hinting at sympathy for the other. Though fighting against the British forces and at the same time preparing for the coming battle with the Arabs, the two organizations were bitter rivals and refused to cooperate. This pattern of deep division seems to have been endemic in Jewish history and was one of the reasons for the final defeat when the Romans subdued Judea 2,000 years ago. (The force was finally disbanded and absorbed into the official

Israeli army in November 1948. There was much opposition to the breakup of this fine military organization with its special history and character. But Prime Minister Ben Gurion was rightly adamant there be only one army and one chain of command.)

When I finally met Menachem Begin, his advice was that because the Irgun had no aircraft, Ezer and I should join the Haganah's air service. Aware of the fierce enmity between the two groups, I realized that Begin was a real statesman and not merely a politician with a short-term view. Relations between the Haganah and the Irgun being so bad, Ezer and I made a pact to keep absolutely secret that we had been members of the Irgun in Europe.

Begin was a short, thin, unremarkable-looking man with spectacles, dapper and always well dressed. At thirty-five, he was some ten years older than Ezer and me and had an almost mystical approach to anything connected with the projected Jewish state. Moments after I met him for the first time, he rose from his chair and, turning to a map of Palestine on the wall of his office, put his open hand on the map and said in a quiet voice, "Oh, our landele, oh, our landele," with such feeling that I was much moved. He was a strange man with an unusual naiveté about mundane matters, which were often elementary to most people. When I told him of the difficulties of flying aircraft to Israel from far away places such as South Africa, he asked, "Can't a big airplane carry a small plane on its back?"

I kept in contact with the Irgun and my former comrades in Paris on a strictly informal friendly basis, inquiring from time to time about what was happening to them. One of these clandestine meetings was with Jacob Meridor. He was put in charge of the Irgun forces in the field when Begin took command of the Irgun. This meeting was not the first contact I had with Meridor.

Meridor had spent two years in British detention camps before he was deported to Gil Gil in Kenya. Though it was possible to escape from Gil Gil, that was only the beginning of the odyssey for the escapee because it was a major problem for a white man to be wandering around Africa without money or resources looking for ways to get to Europe. Meridor had escaped in a way similar to that used by Eliahu Lankin.

Whereas Lankin had managed to reach Europe partly by hiding in the double floor of a bus for some days, Meridor needed help to get out of Africa. During one of my visits to Paris on Irgun business long before coming to Palestine, I had been asked if I would be prepared to fly Meridor out of Kenya. A twin-engine Lockheed Lodestar had been donated by an Irgun sympathizer in Canada and was to be ferried to Paris.

When it arrived, I talked to the ferry pilot. At that time, all my flying had been on single-engine aircraft. The ferry pilot refused to check me out on the Lodestar and there was also a problem with the range. In addition to these difficulties, the whole operation was illegal, and with other problems to be overcome, such as places to land on the way back from Kenya to France, the Irgun in Paris decided to use a professional French pilot. Unaware of the formalities required by the French authorities for crews making their way to Africa and not having prepared themselves for the

French investigations about the flight, the Irgun soon got into trouble and the Lodestar was impounded.

The next development in the saga of getting Meridor out of Africa came when Irgun sympathizers in England located a surplus twin-engine de Havilland Mosquito bomber for sale. I went to inspect the aircraft, but again there was the problem of my getting checked out in this advanced twin, for there was no dual-control Mosquito available. Finally, I persuaded the Irgun to allow me to go to a twin-engine conversion course at Hamble near Southampton, and I got my twin-engine rating.

By this time, the whole operation had become known to the French authorities, and quite possibly the British had learned what we were planning, so we dropped the project. When I had arrived back in Johannesburg after a hasty departure from England at the time of the General Barker fiasco, I arranged with a South African pilot who was an Irgun sympathizer to buy a twin-engine Oxford aircraft for the job. This operation must have been jinxed, because the pilot crashed the aircraft, and we were forced to scrap the whole plan.

Jacob Meridor had been operations officer of the Irgun after escaping from the British banishment center in Kenya and was in Palestine when I arrived in December 1947. Ezer and I were asked to meet him. He told us that the Irgun had acquired three Dakotas, which would be arriving in Palestine shortly, and the Irgun wanted advice about a projected mission for them.

In Egypt a dam was being built on the Nile that was to be the forerunner of the Aswan High Dam. The Irgun thought that destroying the dam would wreak havoc on the Egyptian war effort, and the Irgun wanted to use the Dakotas to bomb the dam. This was an example of the independent and uncoordinated activities of the Irgun and the Haganah at a time before the Irgun was incorporated into the regular forces of the State of Israel. I explained that because the Dakota was not a bomber there was little chance of doing more than minimal damage to the dam wall. Meridor looked at me and in a very matter of fact way said, "Well, then you will just have to dive the two aircraft into the wall of the dam." For a few minutes there was dead silence as the full reality of the proposal sank in.

After the enormity of the proposal sunk in, Ezer and I paled and exchanged glances. We did not continue the conversation, and to this day, I am not sure whether Meridor really intended us to fly into the dam wall. After all we were not Kamikaze pilots. Since that fateful afternoon, I do have some understanding of today's suicide bombers, though I cannot under any circumstances condone such acts. Fortunately, the Dakotas never arrived. I have given much thought to that projected mission and have come to the conclusion that in my frame of mind at the time I might well have agreed to do the job.

THE AIR SERVICE

I enlisted in the air service immediately after coming to Tel Aviv from Haifa. The city was peaceful, and the only danger was from sniping by Jaffa Arabs from the minaret of the

Hassan Bek mosque on the Jaffa side of the border between the two cities. It was a good vantage point from which the snipers could see most of Tel Aviv. In December 1947 Jaffa was an Arab city of some 80,000 inhabitants. Later, the Haganah constructed a large, solid-iron gate across Mea Shearim Street, the main channel through which the bullets were sprayed into the center of Tel Aviv. Apart from that and the shots heard when driving through the orange groves in the vicinity of the city, life was peaceful, although I did sense the awareness and tension of the impending struggle in everyone.

In the beginning I found the harsh sunlight blinding, and I soon learned not to venture out in the morning without sunglasses. The streets, too, were different, much narrower than those I knew, but invariably tree-lined, softening the harshness of the stark white bauhaus buildings.

After the stability and orderliness of the South African environment at that time and the formality that existed there in many ways, the smallness of the Yishuv and the warm intimacy that existed between the people was a revelation to me. It showed itself in many ways: the universal use of first names, the casual dress and lack of ceremony, the directness of speech, and not least, my immediate acceptance into one of the fighting units of the Haganah.

The entire Jewish population of Palestine amounted to a little more than 500,000 people, and we all felt part of one large family, anything happening in the country being of interest to each and every person in a very personal manner. Everyone seemed to know everyone. I am glad to say that despite the population having grown to nearly ten times that number the same feeling of intimacy and closeness underlines life in Israel to this day.

In Tel Aviv there were few signs of a military buildup, though when one passed Café Pinati on Dizengoff Street, one usually saw groups of young men and girls wearing boots and white socks, and white or dark blue shirts. We knew that particular café was the meeting place of the Palmach members, no uniforms and no ranks, but clearly fighting personnel.

Ezer was waiting for me in Tel Aviv and his detailing my experience and background eliminated any difficulties for me in joining the air service. Apart from a few cursory questions about my flying experience, no further details were asked, and I joined Squadron A immediately as one of the pilots. The fact that I was the first and only volunteer at that time from overseas to the air service helped smooth the way.

We were a total of nine operational pilots. A handful had World War II experience; the rest were younger Israelis with only a few hours' flying time. All were former members of the Palmach. Coming from the Palmach, they were highly disciplined fighters but their discipline was unlike that of regular armies. They discharged their duties selflessly without payment. There were no uniforms or ranks or saluting or "sirring," and they required no military code to serve their commanders.

This was my first encounter with the young Sabra (Israeli-born) members of the Palmach. In their sandals and shorts, they were a wholesome bunch, and I was delighted to become one of their number and fly with them. This new generation of Sabras retained the qualities of intelligence and resourcefulness of the Diaspora Jews but without their hang-ups and complexes. I was struck by their lack of pretentiousness, boasting, or conceit. All in all, their being the product of a different environment and culture to mine in the Diaspora, they did not seem strange to me. On the contrary, notwithstanding the superficial differences, I immediately felt close to them like to a brother.

Kibbutzim were well represented among the founding pilots of the air service and were the forerunners of those who later made up the Israel Air Force in the War of Independence of 1948. As these were the pioneers of flying in Israel, who left an indelible stamp on the character of the Israel Air Force, I go into some detail about them:

Eddie Cohen was a South African who joined the Air Service from his kibbutz of Ma'ayan Baruch. Eddie was a former Spitfire pilot in the South African Air Force. He always wore his sheepskin jacket, which carried our signatures on its back. He had come to the kibbutz because of his belief in the need for a Jewish state and the communal values of the kibbutz way of life. I felt close to him because of our flying and South African heritage. Eddie was one of our first casualties. On 29 May 1948, he was shot down by ground fire and killed in the first Messerschmitt operation near Isdud (Ashdod), while attacking an Egyptian armored column approaching from the south and dangerously close to Tel Aviv.

Pinye Ben Porath was a diminutive dark-skinned member of Kibbutz Na'an. He could have been taken for a settler from the Yemen but was of Russian origin. He was a little older than most of us and had a long history as a fighter in the Haganah. He once attacked Arab marauders in the early days of flying before the Air Service's creation. In July 1955, he was killed while flying an El Al Constellation, which inadvertently strayed from its flight path from Zurich to Tel Aviv and was shot down by a Bulgarian fighter near that country's border. Pinye loved the suede desert boots he always wore, and we found them so attractive that we soon followed him to the cobbler on Mercaz Mishari Street. In a matter of days, we were all outfitted with the same handmade boots.

Ya'acov Ben Haim, known to all of us as "Black," was from Kibbutz Kiryat Anavim in the Jerusalem corridor. He was from a family that originated in the Ukraine, and he had the outlook and mannerisms of a farmer, being solid, ponderous, and slow to absorb techniques but very reliable once he absorbed instruction.

Eli Feingersh (later Eli Eyal) was born in Germany and was a member of Kibbutz Sarid in the Jezreel Valley. He was a longtime member of the Palmach, and his opinion carried weight because of his reliability and the analytical way in which he approached our problems.

Pesach (Pussy) Tolchinsky, former U.S. Army Air Force C-47 pilot, was for many years a member of Kibbutz Kfar Giladi in Upper Galilee, and still is.

The pilots who did not originate in kibbutzim were:

Misha Kenner (later Keren), former Strumovik pilot in the Soviet Air Force, who arrived in Israel earlier on an illegal immigrant ship from which he had to jump into the sea and swim ashore. Not having a common language—apart from his Russian and Yiddish and my Hebrew being just more than nonexistent—I soon learned from Misha some juicy swear words in Russian, and we became good friends.

Yitzhak Hennenson, longtime Israeli from Tel Aviv, also of Russian birth, with his ready laugh and eyes twinkling with humor, was one of the more experienced pilots among the young Palestinians.

Ezer Weizman. After I introduced him to the ranks of the Irgun and we later joined the Air Service, we were both conscious of the ideological chasm that divided the Haganah and the Irgun.

PRIMUS IN THE SKY

This mixed team of pilots with its small fleet of aircraft was soon known to us all as "primuses"—the buzz of the small engines sounding like paraffin primus stoves—and they made up the beginnings of the air force. It took months for reinforcement aircrew and aircraft to arrive from abroad. In the meantime, the small band of Air Service pilots managed to hold the fort. In May 1948, when the war began, the major fighting in the air war was carried out by *mahal* (volunteers from abroad)—pilots from the United States, South Africa, Canada, England, and a few other countries.

Most of the local pilots were without operational experience with limited flight time on light aircraft. Among the others, Eddie Cohen had a few hours in fighters of the South African Air Force, Pussy had flown Dakota transports, and Ezer, Thunderbolts, but the war had ended too soon for him to see action. Misha had flown Russian Sturmoviks, but when later on in the war we got Czech Messerschmitt fighters, he couldn't cope with the faster aircraft. That left me as the sole pilot in the Air Service with combat experience. Naturally the young ex-Palmach pilots hoped to graduate to combat planes some day, but, by and large, they were too inexperienced to cope with the unforgiving Messerschmitts we obtained. It is now clear that we shouldn't have expected them to cope with this hybrid. It used a German airframe, Czech engine, and a propeller meant for a bomber, not a fighter. It was altogether a handful even for the experienced pilots who came later as Mahal volunteers and who had flown advanced British and American fighters in World War II.

Sde Dov airfield, in the northern suburbs of Tel Aviv, was our base. There was an assorted collection of civilian aircraft: an Auster, two Tiger Moths, a Taylorcraft, which flew backward at a hint of a headwind, and one luxurious Polish three-seater with the unusual name of RWD 13. This was the nucleus of the future Israel Air Force. Not one of the aircraft boasted an engine larger than 100 horsepower, and they had no armament of any kind.

The field consisted of one east-west runway of 800 meters in a sandy waste on the Mediterranean coast. The sand on which the field was built pervaded our environment completely, and its tawny color is etched into my memory to this day. As Palestine was still a British mandate and no hint of military flying could be shown, we operated from Sde Dov in the guise of a flying club. The field was reached via a dirt road that crossed over a rickety wooden bridge put up by the management of the electric corporation. The corporation charged us a toll of ten piastre each time we crossed the bridge over the narrow Yarkon River. The field was next to the electric-power station with its large chimney. We had one hangar and a tiny wooden hut, which served as our changing room and store for our flying kit. In time, someone appeared without warning and in a true spirit of private enterprise, began to serve us tea and biscuits at a price until someone at headquarters put his foot down and to our regret removed him.

A large, hollow wooden cube painted in black-and-white squares was brought to the field and served as our control tower. Shmuel, a former Belgian Air Force navigator, acted as our flying controller. Not having any radio equipment, he used an Aldis lamp to give us a green for "go" and red for "stop." One mechanic saw to the line maintenance of our small fleet.

We operated entirely clandestinely from Sde Dov. At that time, as the area was still under British mandatory occupation, a British army motor-transport unit used the field as a base. One of my tasks was to shout our identity in English to the British soldier guarding the entrance to the field as we arrived from our billets every morning in a large taxi.

The airfield's single runway ran east to west toward the sea and was also the main approach to the sands on the beach north of Tel Aviv. Quite often, we had to stop takeoffs and landings when a long line of trucks would form to use the runway. They came for the fine building sand near the sea. It was a reminder that we were in the Middle East when we sometimes saw long trains of camels making their way

along the side of the runway from the beach, their saddle-
bags loaded with sacks of sand.

Our billet was in a hostel in north Tel Aviv used for trade
union and kibbutz members who came to the city to study
and to attend seminars. Accommodations were on the second floor of the modern building, usually three or four to a
room. The atmosphere was suffused with the wholesome
feeling of a kibbutz. It was rough but aesthetic, clean and
businesslike and run by old Yishuv Slav types, who had such
an overwhelming impact on the original molding of Israel
and whose influence remains to this day.

After having eaten English breakfasts and prepared meals
all my life at my boarding school and in the SAAF, I was
baffled by my first encounter with the Israeli breakfast in
the dining room. Cold hardboiled eggs, rye bread, which we
had to slice ourselves from the loaf, white cheese, and fresh
vegetables, the latter not served as a salad but in large basins
on the tables. We chose the vegetables we fancied and then
peeled the cucumbers, cut up the peppers and tomatoes,
very communal and kibbutzlike. I made the acquaintance
of a kibbutz custom, the *kolboinik*, into which we threw all
our peels, egg shells, and other debris at the table.

Dizengoff Street was the Champs Elysées of Tel Aviv with
wide sidewalks, al fresco restaurants, and fashionable shops,
but the most characteristic aspect of Dizengoff was and still
is its cafés. During the War of Independence in 1948, one
saw the Palmach girls looking scrubbed and wholesome and
the more fashionable young crowd in Café Rowal. But the
Boheme of Tel Aviv was in Café Kassit, much frequented by
actors and writers. Kassit was chosen by the Air Service as

the aircrew mess where we had our lunch and paid with chits issued by headquarters.

The other residents of our billet were young Sabras, mostly members of the Palmach Pilot's platoon, which had merged with the Air Service on its inception. They accepted me immediately despite my rudimentary knowledge of Hebrew. Fortunately, most of them knew some English, and we managed to communicate in the air without major problems.

My air experience at the time was relatively extensive, having completed air force training and flown nearly fifty combat missions in World War II. For them, I was an experienced operational pilot, and I soon began to teach them whatever I could despite the limitations imposed upon us by the unsuitable aircraft.

As most of the Palmach pilots at that time had managed to gain only about a hundred hours' flying time, they were sorely in need of help and advice. In the Yarden Hotel where I had been moved from the former billets, on many nights after returning from missions and flopping down exhausted on my bed, I was awakened time and again with calls from the field for advice. Those were tough times for me. I was short of sleep after many operational flights under hard conditions, and some nights I was awakened four or five times to make urgent, quick decisions. There was virtually no one to fall back on, for we were desperately short of experienced personnel.

When our operational flights became more frequent, we needed commanders at the airfield and the squadron. This was done in a way typical of the kibbutz culture: we got together and selected commanders by democratic vote. Eli Feingersh was voted the first airfield commander, because he had been the most senior man among those airmen who had been in the Palmach. Shortly after my arrival and being the most experienced airman in the Air Service at that time, I was asked to take command of the squadron and the base at Sde Dov. There were neither ranks nor badges of any kind. The only way of knowing if someone was an officer or in a position of responsibility was if he carried a revolver—a piece of equipment in perennial demand by all.

Early on I was approached on two occasions by a man in army intelligence who asked to borrow my revolver as he said he was scheduled to go out on a dangerous night mission, and I gladly complied, for I was not going to fly on those nights. One night I went to the Park Hotel on Hayarkon Street and saw the intelligence officer on the dance floor wearing my gun. I didn't say a word to him for fear of spoiling the effect of the revolver on his date, but that was the last time he managed to borrow my weapon. On reflection I could have told his girlfriend that he said he borrowed the gun for a dangerous mission that night.

We carried out many other types of missions for the Air Service, as in the case of Moshe Shertok (later Sharett), who became the first foreign minister of Israel. He had returned from a mission to the United States, and because there had been shooting on the road from the Lydda Airport now known as Lod, it was dangerous for him to travel by car. I was asked to fly to Lydda to meet him and fly him to Tel Aviv. Before leaving for the airfield, which was still in the hands of the British, I was given a hand grenade.

Being a newcomer to such weapons, I was given only a stun grenade, which I put into my trouser pocket. After landing at Lydda, I was searched by a British policeman. I knew he touched and felt the grenade in my pocket, but he did not react perhaps out of fear of involvement with Irgun "terrorists." I can well understand the anxiety of the Haganah about all traffic to Lydda, for we had to take care when flying out of the confines of Tel Aviv, and we were regularly shot at from the village of Yahudia near the airport.

CHAPTER FIVE

First Missions

NIGHT FLIGHTS

O F all the places to which we flew in Israel in early 1948, I found the Dead Sea area the most unusual and the most mysterious. It is named "Dead" because its bitter salt waters cannot support any form of life. It is a large expanse of water more than a thousand feet below sea level, the lowest place on earth, in a wild, dry gash, which is unexpectedly relieved by the sight of the blue water.

The sparkling blue of the water seen from the air provides a welcome contrast to the total aridity of the desert surroundings but the blueness is deceptive because the water is saturated with chemicals to such an extent that one can float effortlessly in the water. The dry, hot climate with temperatures reaching 45 degrees Centigrade makes it hard to withstand the conditions for long. I felt a wary respect for the Dead Sea area when I first landed, a respect bordering on uneasiness. This same feeling remains with me to this day, which I find inexplicable and mysterious, possibly because of the biblical warnings about Sodom and Gomorrah.

The Dead Sea Potash Works are based at Sdom at the southern tip of the Dead Sea. Many of my flights in the early days of my flying operations in Israel were to that area. The founder and main shareholder of the potash company was a former Russian called Novomeysky, small in stature but large in imagination and foresight. Shortly after the turn of the twentieth century, he had foreseen the potential of the salts in the Dead Sea and had formed a pioneer company to extract Potash to sell worldwide. I had to fly him back to Tel Aviv from Sdom. I landed close to the Dead Sea and saw the diminutive Mr. Novomeysky waiting for me. He looked at the decrepit little RWD 13, minus its right-hand door, for we had started throwing packages from our laps to settlements cut off from the rest of the Yishuv. He was clearly not impressed. Fortunately, it was late afternoon, the air was smooth, and I brought him to Tel Aviv after a pleasant flight. He kept glancing down worriedly out of the missing door, however, and I am sure he never forgot that flight with the young pilot who could not even carry on a conversation with him in Hebrew.

In time I flew many sorties to Sdom to evacuate women and other noncombatants and to fly in various army personnel. The Palmach had a strong presence there, and I was ordered to fly their commander to Sdom. Gen. Yitzhak Sadeh, well known and loved, was the first commander of the Palmach and one of its founders. In World War I, he had served in the Russian army and had been decorated for bravery. His involvement in military affairs in the early days of the Yishuv had been continuous from the time of the 1936 riots. He was a maverick in military thinking, and he was the spirit behind the doctrine of breaking out of strongholds and vigorously attacking the enemy in the open, a tactic not employed before he took command.

At one time, he had also been the acting chief of the Haganah and was well known as the teacher and commander of most of Israel's senior officers. I had not met him before. He was later to lead the forces that successfully defended Kibbutz Mishmar Ha'emek in the Jezreel Valley and routed the attacking Arab Liberation Army in April 1948 despite being outnumbered nearly ten to one. Sadeh used brilliant tactics, containing the enemy forces in their frontal attack while deftly cutting all their lines of communication. The stunning victory at Mishmar Ha'emek heartened the people of Israel greatly at that time of deep anxiety. One of Tel Aviv's main thoroughfares today bears his name.

Sadeh arrived at Sde Dov shortly before I was to take off for Sdom, a tall, bulky man in his customary khaki shorts and shirt. His spectacles gave him a studious appearance despite his powerful physique, resulting from his past as a wrestler and weight lifter. I seated him next to me and we took off. It was in the early afternoon, and as usual at that time of day it was turbulent with thermals and broken cloud in the Negev area. We were tossed around violently, and we needed our seat belts during the whole flight. I noticed that Sadeh was sitting quietly, from time to time turning away from me with his handkerchief pressed to his face. When we landed, I understood why he had been so silent.

He had spent most of the flight vomiting unobtrusively into his handkerchief without saying a word to me.

After the United Nations decided to partition Palestine into two separate entities, one Jewish and one Arab, terrorist activities by the Arab irregular forces increased greatly. My squadron at Sde Dov carried the entire load of flight operations. With our limited roster of aircraft and pilots, we flew day and night, trying to keep up with requests for help pouring in from Haganah headquarters. By the end of December 1947, the situation began to heat up further with increased violence from the irregular Arab units. We had to fly many reconnaissance sorties over Arab positions. They began to shoot at our aircraft, at that time only with small arms. Regardless, we continued our flights, often the only method of transport and communication between the settlements and the center of the country. To say that our equipment was unsuited to the missions is a gross understatement; we had badly maintained aircraft, in most cases no radio communication, inadequate instruments, unsuitable maps, and not one parachute. I noted the growing strain on the young pilots, most of whom had only limited flight experience, and saw that some of them were reaching breaking point. Accordingly, I instituted a shift system for all aircrew, twenty-four hours on duty and twenty-four hours rest. It helped.

One flight illustrates the conditions under which we operated. Flying the Polish RWD back from a Negev sortie in the late afternoon with my Russian comrade Misha Kenner, I was delayed at Nir Am, the Jewish stronghold near Gaza with its narrow landing strip. After takeoff and while head-

ing for our home base at Sde Dov, it was getting dark. With
no equipment for night flying nor even instrument lights, I
asked Misha sitting next to me to light a match from time
to time near the airspeed indicator. He did so, but when it
became completely dark and the matches began to run out,
he became very agitated. I managed to fly on a more or less
even keel in the darkness by reference to occasional lights
on the ground. After a while the lights of Tel Aviv appeared
in the distance and when I landed without much difficulty
on our strip at Sde Dov, Misha became calmer.

One morning, Misha failed to return on schedule from a
local flight in the Tiger Moth. I went out on a search for
him and eventually found the Tiger not very far from Sde
Dov. He had made a forced landing after running out of
fuel near Sidni Ali, the mosque of an Arab village some
twenty-five kilometers from our base. From my vantage
point circling above the mosque which is perched on a cliff
near the sea, I could see a huge crowd of Arabs, some hundreds clearly identified by their galabiyas and white Kefa
headresses, surrounding a seated figure near the wall of the
mosque. I knew it was Misha.

The Tiger appeared undamaged, obviously having made
a good forced landing. I continued circling at low altitude
in the hope that my presence would discourage any attempt
to harm him. When Misha finally stood up and gave a non-
chalant wave to me, I had to decide whether to try a landing
to try to extricate him or to return to base and request assistance from the ground forces. I decided not to try and fight
it out there and then, though I buzzed the crowd by swoop-
ing down at ground level. At that time, the military situa-

tion was so unsettled that I did not know if our ground forces would manage to reach him. We had no radios, so I decided it would be wiser to return to base and get help.

My decision proved to be right. The mob had no violent intentions, and a Haganah unit sent to the scene had no difficulty in persuading them to let Misha take off in the Tiger. When I questioned Misha later about the incident, asking him how he communicated with the Arabs, he said, "No problem. When the mob surrounded me, I pointed to the aircraft and motioned the crowd to back away shouting, "Benzine, whoosh!" It worked.

We made many flights to maintain contact with kibbutzim, sometimes dropping messages. Later we carried army walkie-talkie sets, enabling us to report on Arab troop movements. In many cases we were the sole means of transporting army commanders or reinforcements from kibbutz to kibbutz, and dropping supplies of ammunition.

An important part of our duties was the supervision of the water pipelines, the only source of water supply to the Negev kibbutzim after having been isolated from the rest of the country by the Arabs. Irregular Arab forces constantly blew up sections of the pipeline. From the air we would see large pools of water in the desert and alerted the Haganah who sent repair teams. Another part of our duties was to drop daily newspapers to the surrounded settlements, along with chocolate bars. We were a great morale booster to the lonely and beleaguered kibbutz settlers, and when necessary, we flew badly wounded kibbutzniks to hospitals.

In time those kibbutzim cut off from the rest of the Yishuv and devised a system to ensure that their needs were

being attended to satisfactorily. They began to appoint
"consuls." One kibbutz member was sent to stay in Tel Aviv
and to represent that particular kibbutz. They used to bad-
ger us with requests for various kinds of assistance, be it the
supply of medications or ammunition or rifles. One or two
of the consuls were invariably to be seen at Sde Dov before
our takeoff on a mission, and they often tried to join the
crew.

One night at Sde Dov in October 1948 with the moon
shining strongly and the stars glittering in the sky, we
loaded a DC-3 we had obtained from the South African airline Westair, which I had formed shortly before. We used
the aircraft for missions after they landed from Johannesburg on normal flights before flying back to Johannesburg.
Revivim had a small strip, which we sometimes used for
flying in light supplies and relief personnel but which was
too short for landing a large machine like the DC-3. It was
the outpost closest to the border with Egypt and far to the
south of Beersheba. It was one of the most exposed loca-
tions in the country.

A consul named Michael, a blue-eyed German Jew, his
fair complexion burned red by the harsh sun of Israel, approached me. He was a member of Kibbutz Revivim in the
southern part of the Negev near the Egyptian border. While
we loaded the aircraft and briefed the crew, Michael begged
me to let him join the flight. He wouldn't be able to speak
to his family or his friends in the kibbutz, but he would at
least be able to see the settlement and gauge their chances
of surviving the attack we knew would come from the Egyptian army after the end of the mandate. We knew that Re-

vivim was a prime target they had to overcome in their advance into Palestine. I had misgivings, but Michael begged to go, trying to persuade me that he knew the area and could help the crew find the settlement as well as the best point at which to drop the supplies. Finally, I agreed.

After takeoff I remained at the field awaiting their return. We waited for more than two hours, but the DC-3 did not arrive. Long after its estimated time of arrival back at Sde Dov, we began to worry. Eventually we received a communication from Southern Command that the aircraft was shot down by ground fire in the northern Negev, and the occupants, including Michael, perished. The exact circumstances remain unknown to this day, but I still see him in my mind's eye as night after night he followed the crews tirelessly while they prepared their craft for the flights to the Negev.

UMM RASHRASH

In December 1947 I made the longest flight I have ever flown in a small aircraft in one day. The tiny British Auster is no bigger than the better-known Piper Cub and was our workhorse at Sde Dov. My mission was to survey the southern and southeastern borders as far as the Red Sea. I took a former Soviet army tank expert, who was to examine the feasibility of introducing an armored column from the Far East via the Red Sea, then advance from the far south to the center of the country. I believe there was a plan to equip a unit in the Far East with World War II war-surplus tanks from the Philippines, and after docking at the shore near the present port of Eilat, it was to make its way up the Arava Valley to the north.

From Tel Aviv we flew to Kibbutz Revivim in the Negev to refuel from jerry-cans carried in the aircraft, and from there to the extreme south along the border with Transjordan. In the southern Negev in 1947, we held only five positions: the kibbutzim of Gvulot, Beit Eshel, Tse'elim, Hatserim, and Revivim. Revivim was the most southern, near the Egyptian border. The kibbutzniks had cleared a short strip in the desert.

I spotted the kibbutz easily, the only green area in a landscape burned brown by the sun and no moisture. Rain falls rarely in the cruel desert of the southern Negev.

I spent some time studying the nearly featureless maps of the uninhabited deep south of Palestine. After taking off we climbed to cross the escarpment before descending down below sea level to the desolate valley of the Arava.

As soon as we saw Ein Husub (now Ein Hatseva) the first of the oases in the Arava, I descended and flew low above the dry stony desert ground. From Ein Husub we followed the track that vaguely marked the route from Aqaba to the Dead Sea. In biblical times, long before the sea route through the Suez Canal, this was the main route from the Red Sea through Palestine to Europe. On the way we examined and made notes of the location and appearance of the five existing oases, whose points were not well marked. Only a few date palms and a hint of green indicated their location. We continued at low level to Aqaba near present-day Eilat. I am not sure whether my passenger was unfamiliar with Hebrew or if he was just a silent type, but whatever the reason we hardly exchanged a word during the nine-hour flight.

All that could be seen in the Arava was the stony landscape with a little scrub vegetation and an occasional oasis. Our only company for more than three hours was the mountain range of Moab and Edom on our left, brooding over us as we made our way along the Arava. On the right, the sharp, high crags of the Sinai Mountains added to the wild and inhospitable feel of a landscape stark and devoid of any sign of human habitation. I wondered at the courage of Moses and his flock, wandering for forty years in that terrible terrain to escape Egyptian slavery more than 2,000 years ago.

Finally, the coast of the Red Sea was in the distance, a refreshing change from the dryness of the environment surrounding us on all sides. We circled low above Umm Rash-rash, forerunner of today's Eilat. There was little to be seen apart from two elongated gray blocks of the British police post, and there was no sign of life apart from a few camels and some Arabs on horses. After circling the forlorn police post, I was eager to leave the godforsaken stretch of coast and head for home.

ETZION BLOC

Sometimes, we flew to Gush Etzion, a group of five kibbutzim in the midst of the large Arab area between Jerusalem and Hebron. There was no other Jewish settlement or village for many kilometers. The kibbutzim were about a kilometer apart, so planned because of the danger from the Arabs surrounding them. The few hundred courageous settlers possessed only a handful of machine guns and rifles for their protection. Already by December 1947, they were surrounded and cut off from the rest of the Yishuv. The only way to them was through Arab villages. An attempt had been made in the middle of January 1948 to reinforce and supply them from Jerusalem, but the thirty-five men in the rescue party, to this day well recorded in Israeli history as the "Lamed Heh"(thirty-five in Hebrew), were butchered to a man by Arab irregulars. By the time I had contact with the kibbutzim, they were under daily attack by Arab irregulars and were short of medical supplies and ammunition. Fortunately, all the children and some of the women had been evacuated.

A few weeks after the "Lamed Heh" were killed, we received reports that a large force under the guerrilla leader Abdel Kader el Husseini was heading for the group of settlements. A reconnaissance by one of our planes confirmed many vehicles heading toward the area. The gravity of the situation owing to the severe lack of ammunition and medical supplies made it essential to provide urgent assistance. After losing the Lamed Heh platoon, it was clear there was no way of bringing reinforcements or supplies by road. We agreed to try to supply them by air.

After receiving the order from the GHQ in the afternoon, we made an operational plan using three aircraft, the major part of our air resources. I agreed to fly the Tiger Moth twenty or thirty feet above the target area before and during the proposed drop—quite a dangerous project to fly at low level over firing troops in the tiny Tiger Moth. Eli Eyal in the front cockpit was to fire a Bren gun, and both of us would hurl hand grenades to keep the enemy heads down. Ezer and Hennenson in the Auster and Black and Pussy in the RWD 13 would drop the ammunition and medical supplies.

On a cold midwinter morning on 15 January 1948, we drove out to the airfield. At that hour Tel Aviv was quiet with virtually no traffic. The calm appearance of the city contrasted with the tension I felt as we drove through the deserted streets. At the field, Eli checked the Bren gun and the hand grenades before we took off just before dawn. With Eli in the front cockpit, the Bren gun on his lap, we climbed to cruising altitude and turned toward the range of mountains to the east. The other two aircraft followed some minutes later as we headed toward the besieged kibbutzim. This was to be their last contact with the Yishuv.

After a short flight in the freezing open cockpit, the green valleys of the plains gave way to the stony foothills of the ancient forbidding Judean mountains looming over the coastal plain. As we approached Kfar Etzion, we saw the mountains were covered by low cloud. After breaking through a gap in the clouds, we were able to make out the five groups of kibbutz buildings set in a defensive circle. The big Arab city of Hebron is to the south, Bethlehem to the north. Nearer to them but not too close were villages containing thousands of hostile Arabs. The entire area looked dry and inhospitable, the only patches of green being in the kibbutzim. I was full of admiration for the brave settlers

with their families who had come to settle those stony hills
buttressed by their faith that their return to the land of their
fathers was ordained thousands of years ago.

Eli's Bren gun jammed after one test round, and because
of the lack of communication between us, because I knew
almost no Hebrew and Eli knew little English, I couldn't
make out what had happened. We continued to shout
loudly to each other through the primitive speaking tube,
but I had difficulty in understanding anything apart from
the word "kaput."

I decided to continue the mission with the intention of
at least buzzing the enemy troops during the drop. Eli continued shouting to me through the tube intercom, but with
the buffeting of the wind I could not make out what he was
trying to tell me. Fortunately, there were no hostile forces
at that hour in the immediate vicinity of the kibbutzim, and
the other two aircraft were able to drop their supplies on
the rubber tires, which had been spread out to receive them.

As we flew over at low level, the kibbutzniks rushed out
to wave in relief and gratitude. I felt satisfaction and a closeness to our embattled brethren down below encircled and
lonely but not forsaken, with us as their only contact with
the rest of the Yishuv and perhaps their sole instrument of
survival. The depth of emotion I felt during the missions to
help them has not been matched before or since. I have
helped other beseiged kibbutzim, but Kfar Etzion remains
etched in my memory, secured by some bond perhaps because of the hopelessness of their situation and their lonely
stand against overwhelming odds.

After making the drop, we saw another aircraft that had joined us over Kfar Etzion. It did not take long for us to realize it was a British reconnaissance Auster. We beat a hasty retreat, making for Kibbutz Be'erot Yitzhak while throwing out all incriminating evidence, and from there we made for Sde Dov. Later we heard that the British pilot reported that he had been fired on by "Jewish aircraft." What had happened was that he had seen a puff of exhaust smoke from one of our engines and thought we had fired at him. After our return and hearing that we were supposed to have fired on the British aircraft, we decided that for the investigation by the British police authorities we would admit to having been flying near Kfar Etzion while dropping medical supplies to the wounded settlers.

We met that evening and discussed the pros and cons of what might happen to whoever said they had been in the air above Etzion. Having recently been an officer in an RAF squadron, it would have been unwise for me to have even divulged that I was flying in Palestine at that time. Each one of us had one problem or another. Some had spent time in British detention camps while others were on the British black list as members of the underground movements.

We agreed unanimously that Ezer should say that he had been flying there at that time. He was one of the few local pilots who had a valid flying license and he carried the name Weizman, certainly an acceptable name to the British because of his uncle Chaim Weizmann.

A few hours later, Ezer reported to the police and spent the night in custody. I was worried about him and visited the Tel Aviv police station in Rehov Hashahar the next morning. I found him sitting and chatting contentedly with the police guards, a cup of Turkish coffee in his hand. He was released the next day. An amusing sequel to the incident was that one of the English newspapers printed a headline to the effect that "Dr. Chaim Weizmann had fired on a British officer from a Jewish plane in Palestine." Chaim Weizmann threatened to sue the paper, which retracted its report and paid libel damages. Kfar Etzion continued to withstand heavy attacks, but the situation was hopeless. On 14 May 1948, the Arab Legion breached the defenses, and the mobs of irregulars who followed the troops into the settlements butchered most of the men and women settlers. The final chapter of their heroic resistance ended in a bloodbath. The wounded together with most of the women, eighty in all, were sheltering in a bunker. The officers of the Arab Legion did not try to control their troops, who swarmed into the kibbutz for the final slaughter. They grabbed one of the girls in the bunker and pushed a grenade into her hand. After pulling out the pin, they tried to make her throw it into the bunker. She refused, so one of the mob threw the grenade into the bunker below them, killing most of the remaining kibbutzniks.

CHAPTER SIX

Airplanes and Volunteers

DOUBLE PUSHKIN

THE Kfar Etzion mission was our first real "combined operation," and though limited both in its scope and effectiveness, it was the first of a number of military air actions that we carried out under the difficult conditions of the time.

Already in December 1947, Arab guerrillas had started crossing the borders of Palestine in preparation for the ending of the British mandate. More than 600 crossed in December from Syria and Lebanon, and a Syrian army regiment departed from Damascus in preparation for the border crossing. In this threatening climate, the air service took desperate measures to support the ill-equipped kibbutzim and settlements.

We formed a unit to drop bombs by hand from our aircraft. At first we used 15-kilo and 20-kilo bombs, but later 25-kilo and 50-kilo bombs. Our nickname for the 25-kilo model was "Pushkin," and the 50-kilo bombs, "Double Pushkin." The origin of these strange names may be from the shouted pilot's instructions in English to "push" them out. The bombs were fitted with a sturdy iron handle and in some cases were armed by pulling a fuse before throwing them out of the aircraft, often from our laps.

This was accompanied with a bang and a smell of cordite, an unpleasant experience especially when flying alone in a small airplane at night. The bombing campaign was directed mostly at the enemy's morale and was effective especially at night when, after the bombing, we dropped empty soft-drink bottles, which made an eerie whistle followed by a deathly silence when landing on sandy soil.

In time, we improved our methods of dropping supplies to beleaguered settlements by using small parachutes and cardboard containers with winglets that opened during their descent. Although some of the drops were successful, however, many missed their targets.

In early 1948 we succeeded in buying nineteen surplus Austers from local British army stock. These aircraft were not in flying condition and were transported by road from the RAF base in Aqir to a hideout in Sarona in Tel Aviv. They were regarded as scrap, so when we managed by cannibalization to get some of them into flying condition, illegally of course, we painted the same registration number of our sole official Auster VQ-PAS on *all* of them. Under each machine's tail, we painted our own small registration number, for example, VQ-PAS 1 or 2, and so on.

PURCHASE AND RECRUIT

After the Kfar Etzion operation, I became desperate to do something to improve our aircraft situation, knowing, too, that our ground troops and naval forces were in a similar situation. In January 1948 Air Service headquarters agreed to my urging that I should go at my own expense to South Africa to try to buy aircraft and to recruit experienced pilots. I left for Johannesburg on 15 February 1948, confident the committed Jewish community in South Africa would do all in its power to assist.

It was strange for me to return to my parents' home. I was back in the environment in which I had grown up, and everything was just as it had been before I left. Yet, I was now only a visitor, my roots already replanted 10,000 miles away in Palestine.

In Johannesburg I went to the Zionist Federation offices armed with an imposing letter from the General Council for Jewish Aviation, a mythical organization which neither I or anyone else had heard of. Coming from a well-known Zionist family that was for many years a major supporter of the cause of a national home, doors were opened and I was immediately offered help.

My problem was not so much finding people ready and qualified to serve with us but to buy aircraft and deliver them to Palestine secretly in the face of the British arms embargo. That would let us survive until the hoped-for illegal armada of aircraft arrived from the United States.

I, therefore, worked at breakneck pace and exhorted everyone else to do the same so that we could survive until then. The pressure I felt to get some aircraft quickly to Palestine in time for the expected ending of the mandate guided my every waking moment and left me no time for any other activity. Shortly after starting my work there I insisted that the federation offices go on to a quasi-wartime schedule working seven days a week, and no one raised any objection. I made it clear to them that if the planes did not get to Palestine almost immediately, we would not survive.

Evidently, the Jewish authorities in Palestine heard complaints about my insisting on the introduction of emergency measures in the daily routine at the Zionist Federation in Johannesburg. South African Jewry, committed though it was to the cause of Israel, was quite unaware of the desperate situation of the Yishuv and, in particular, of the Air Service. After a few days of frantic activity, the head of the Zionist Federation in Johannesburg told me he had received a message from Ben Gurion in Palestine complaining about the problems my activities were causing the Jewish community in Johannesburg. I was hauled over the coals by Ben Gurion after my arrival back in Tel Aviv, but nothing further was done about the so-called tension I caused for the Jewish community.

In the Zionist Federation offices in Johannesburg, I was astonished to find a recruiting section operating with the names of thousands of volunteers who were ready to go to Palestine to help in the battle we all knew was coming. There were pilots, navigators, and air gunners, as well as technical personnel with experience in engines and airframes, radar, and electronics. There were others who had no military experience but were keen to help in the defense of the coming Jewish State.

It is surprising that there were so many volunteers in a small community totaling just over a hundred thousand Jews in South Africa. In the 1948 War of Independence, this community provided more than 800 volunteers, not many less than those who came from the great Jewish community of 5.5 million in the United States. My explanation is the deep roots of the South African Jews in their strongly Zionist Lithuanian past, whereas the Jews of the United States tended to focus more around the synagogue and Judaism.

There were so many volunteers that I found it hard to make a selection. I made it clear that there would be no pay, only board and lodging and a few pounds a month for pocket money. I believe this policy obviated many of the problems that later arose among volunteers from other countries who had erroneously been promised substantial salaries.

From the many suitable applicants, I chose several pilots and two navigators, all with distinguished records from World War II. As the priority was the purchase of aircraft— and it was no use bringing large numbers of aircrew and other personnel until we had enough aircraft—I kept the numbers down to fewer than twenty. I could easily have recruited more than a thousand if we could have found use for them. Some of those I selected arrived in Palestine by flying the aircraft I had purchased, and the rest came later by airliner.

The difficulties of buying aircraft and getting them to Palestine were enormous because of South African law and the United States and British arms embargo. As a start I rented a Cessna and flew to the strips where surplus wartime aircraft were being auctioned by the South African Department of Defence.

I took a mechanic named Haim with me to check whatever we would find. On arrival at an air base near the city of Kimberley, I was astonished to see for sale fifty Kittyhawk fighters identical to the ones I flew in 250 Squadron, all in good condition with their engines cocooned. Not having seen a Kittyhawk since the squadron in Italy three years before, I was moved speechless with nostalgia. The aircraft were lined up almost surrealistically in precise rows and looked as if they were ready to take off for a raid on a target in northern Italy.

The buyers at the auction were mostly Jewish scrap dealers who guessed what I was up to. Some of them came to me clearly moved and told me that they had arranged the bidding so as to let me buy the aircraft cheaply. The planes were considered scrap metal by the government. After Haim and I made a cursory inspection, I entered the bidding and in no time was the owner of fifty fine wartime fighters at a price of six pounds each!

Now came the difficult part, how to smuggle them into Palestine in the face of the embargo or, even more difficult, how to fly or to transport them to Palestine. I was well aware that there would be no help on the long, hard flight of 10,000 kilometers up Africa through the Islamic nations of Sudan and Egypt.

I explored all possible avenues, including one involving dismantling the Kittyhawks and loading them into large cargo Bristol Wayfarers in which we could fly them to Palestine illegally. This idea had its roots in the job I had done a year before, transporting the Irgun bomb expert Yoel illegally to England from Paris via unannounced landings on the way.

In retrospect I feel that I gave up on the Kittyhawk project too soon, but I was overwhelmed by the difficulties and realized that the whole undertaking would involve more time than we had. Our immediate needs in the squadron at Sde Dov were so pressing that it was vital to bring reinforcements of some kind to the squadron immediately. Even light civilian aircraft that would be much simpler to get through to Palestine would help to save the day. In the end, the difficulties proved to be insurmountable for we could find no way to load the fighters onto a ship under the noses of the police, and we had to leave the P-40s to the scrap dealers. How changed the map of Israel might have been if I had succeeded in getting those fifty modern Kittyhawk fighters to Palestine by May 1948 at the start of the war!

I felt that the problem of obtaining real military aircraft was longer term. I was convinced—wrongly as it turned out—that military aircraft would be arriving in quantity from the United States as soon as the British left Palestine. I knew that whatever arrangements I made for the Kittyhawks would involve much time and would probably end up as a nonstarter. My worry about the comrades I had left behind in the squadron virtually without airworthy planes made it imperative to get even civilian aircraft to Palestine. They would have to fly out of South Africa, ostensibly to Europe, and somehow disappear on their way to Palestine.

It was, therefore, necessary to choose aircraft capable of flying all the way to Palestine, and they had to be suitable for conversion to military duties. After an arduous search in South Africa, I found that nothing was available apart from a few Fairchild Argus high-wing monoplanes. They were similar to the Austers, and I knew it would be easy for our younger pilots to convert to them. The Fairchilds' same high-wing configuration afforded good visibility for reconnaissance, and they were bigger and more powerful than our Austers. I decided that they should be flown to Palestine in open formation with an experienced captain leading them in a larger aircraft equipped with radio communications. This radio equipment was mandatory for any light aircraft crossing the Sudan. Accordingly, I bought a de Havilland Rapide twin-engine biplane and hired a professional pilot and a wireless operator to lead them on the flight with ten stops for refueling.

The need to have a registered owner who would not create suspicion was conveniently solved by arranging with Pan African Air Charter (a local nonscheduled carrier) to register them under their flag. That would hopefully fend off questions about three single-engine Fairchilds making their way up the continent of Africa. The route was from Johannesburg through the largely uncharted territories of the Rhodesias, Tanganyika, Kenya, the Sudan, and Egypt. Then, they would have to disappear. Pan African was owned by British Jews, and after I explained the setup to them, they obligingly agreed to cooperate by allowing us to fly the Fairchilds out of South Africa under their flag.

In the meantime, I contacted Beechcraft in the United States and ordered two of their Bonanza four-seater luxury touring aircraft, which were delivered to me in Johannesburg in a few weeks. Shortly thereafter I bought five DC-3s, a second de Havilland Rapide, and a twin-engine Anson light bomber. Registration of the rest of the planes was as follows: one Bonanza Beechcraft appeared as my personal aircraft and the second was registered as the property of Cyril Katz, the volunteer whom I had chosen to fly it to Palestine. He had flown C-47s in the South African Air Force, and I was sure he could make the long flight. Throughout the entire period, I found and purchased planes. I was careful not even to mention the subject over the telephone. Thus, we managed to keep our activities unknown to the South African authorities.

The next step after the widening of the Anglo-U.S. embargo to include civilian aircraft in April 1948 was to form a charter nonscheduled company in Johannesburg, which we called Westair, to register the C-47s. In May 1948, this charter company became Universal Airlines and began a twice-weekly service to Israel. Most of its passengers were former South African army and air force veterans who had volunteered to join the Jewish forces in Palestine. Westair became a vital link between South Africa and Palestine. Moreover, while on their normal passenger runs, the C-47s were used, after their arrival in Palestine, to fly urgent supplies to beleaguered kibbutzim during their turnaround. After the war, Universal became part of Israel's national carrier El Al.

Unknown to most, including the South African government to this day, one of the C-47s even carried out a night bombing raid on Damascus while it had large South African registration letters on its fuselage and wings. The Anson went by the West African route but crashed en route. The rest of the aircraft purchased in South Africa eventually arrived in Palestine. They tripled the entire fleet of planes we had in the air service when I left for Johannesburg on 15 February 1948.

LUSAKA

The South African government appeared to ignore our activities, and we were able to operate largely without hindrance throughout the fateful year of 1948. Despite this I soon became of much interest to the special branch of the South African Police Department. I realized it was essential to get the airplanes out of the country as soon as possible, and, after I decided to be the first to make the journey to Palestine, I left in late April in one Bonanza while Cyril accompanied me in another Bonanza. We cleared customs at Pietersburg on the northern border of South Africa after submitting flight plans for Lusaka in northern Rhodesia, now Zambia.

During the flight I was puzzled that when the northern Transvaal Mountains and valleys gave way to bush and scrub there was no sign of human habitation for hundreds of miles. Though the countryside looked fertile and well watered, I could make out only a very occasional desolate-looking village of round African huts with straw or grass roofs.

I discovered later that this part of Africa was a prohibited area for flying as it is a zone of sleeping sickness, the scourge of Africa. I was later reprimanded by the Rhodesian Civil Aviation authorities for using that route, and they set up a board of inquiry. During the exhaustive investigation, we did not disclose our true destination and they accepted our story that we were on our way to England.

After a three-and-a-half-hour flight in the turbulent midday heat, I landed at Lusaka. When I refueled, I discovered that the auxiliary fuel tank installed in the cabin had collapsed because of faulty installation in Johannesburg. Because of the long distance from Wadi Halfa in the Sudan to Tel Aviv, I had ordered long-range tanks to be flown in from the United States and hurriedly installed in the Bonanzas in Johannesburg. Because I was always urging everyone connected with the operation to complete the job quickly, I felt partly to blame for their having neglected to remove a seal on the pipe leading from the tank to the engine. When the pump drew fuel, it created a strong underpressure because of the sealed air inlet pipe. This meant that I could not fly nonstop from Wadi Halfa to Palestine but would have to refuel at Luxor in Egypt. This was not a very desirable route through a hostile country, which was already giving support to the Arab irregular forces and was fated eventually to become Israel's most powerful enemy. But I had no alternative.

In the meantime, Cyril was nowhere to be seen though his Bonanza was a trifle faster than mine. After two hours of anxious waiting, a message came, delivered part of the way by an African with a note in a cleft stick. It informed me that Cyril had landed at a strip in the jungle near the Zambezi River and couldn't take off because his flaps didn't work.

The maintenance engineer of Central African Airways in Lusaka graciously agreed to accompany me with his bag of

tools to fly to Cyril. I found the strip at Chirundu by the
Zambezi River in wild country. In that area there is neither
habitation nor any sign of human life, and Cyril was very
relieved to see me. He said he had lost his way while airsick
from the turbulence he had encountered. We couldn't fix
the flaps, and I decided we should leave for Salisbury (now
Harare) about an hour's flight away to get help.

The three of us climbed into my Bonanza, and I taxied to
the end of the strip. As it was a short strip, I opened to full
throttle with my feet firmly on the brakes to lessen the distance required for takeoff, then released the brakes. I sensed
something was wrong but kept the throttle fully open to get
flying speed as quickly as possible while holding the stick in
the pit of my stomach to lift the nose.

Suddenly the nose lurched down and hit the ground and
the propeller smashed. We ended up in an almost vertical
position, but we were unhurt. It seems that the surface had
given way and the nose-wheel of the Bonanza had sunken
deeply into the ground. We realized that the strip was covered with sun-baked mud and that underneath the thin
layer of hard surface was a deep bed of mud because of our
proximity to the river.

We left a black ranger to guard the aircraft and struck out
for Salisbury in a truck. After a while, we were surprised to
discover a police post not far away. We spent the night in
that wild and desolate part of Africa in the police post with
a few black rangers. We were in the malaria belt, but having
taken anti-malaria pills, we thought that we were reasonably
safe.

As night came we began to hear the cacophony of jungle

night noises. I heard the roaring of lions close by and the trumpeting of elephants. I was worried about the aircraft parked on the deserted strip nearby, but it would have been foolhardy to venture out of the police post at night. We tried to get some sleep on the floor, and at first light, we made our way to the strip. There we saw monkeys climbing happily all over the aircraft but more worrying were the traces of elephant dung close to the planes. The visits had evidently been made by the elephants with great care in pitch darkness. The trumpeting of the elephants we heard during the night had been from farther away. Again, we found a ranger to guard the aircraft and started out for Salisbury.

In Salisbury I organized a local aircraft company to repair the two Bonanzas, and eventually they were brought to the city by road. Mine was badly damaged because the engine had lifted itself off its bearers. Cyril's aircraft was eventually made serviceable by a Rhodesian company and was later flown to Palestine. Mine arrived only after the war was over.

LUXOR

I returned to Johannesburg by train, where I woke up in the morning with a splitting headache and a high temperature. A doctor diagnosed malignant malaria, and I spent a week in bed delirious and disoriented. So the anti-malaria pills had not managed to protect me from the mosquitoes in the jungles of the Zambezi. The failure of the mission didn't help my mood. As soon as I could get out of bed, I ordered another Bonanza. Finance for all aircraft purchases and

other costs came without any difficulty or questions from
the South African Zionist Federation.

By now the South African police were watching my every
step, and I felt it likely they would impound my second aircraft if I tried to leave with it for Palestine. I asked Cecil
Wulfsohn, an experienced pilot who had flown the Cairo-
Johannesburg route many times during World War II, to fly
the Bonanza out of the country for me. We linked him with
a young lady of an Afrikaans family having close connections to the establishment in South Africa as a kind of partner or paramour. The ruse worked. They departed without
problems.

Cecil handed the plane over to me in Rhodesia after getting it out of South Africa, and I continued on the flight to
Palestine. The route crossed the whole continent of Africa,
a distance of more than 10,000 kilometers of savannah ending over uninhabited and largely uncharted deserts. Anyone
undertaking this flight, in addition to maps, must be well
equipped with water, food, hand compass, anti-malaria tab-
lets, and some kind of weapon for self-defense.

The route over Zimbabwe (formerly Rhodesia), Tanzania
(formerly Tanganyika), Kenya, Sudan, Egypt, and finally the
Sinai Desert meant five days of solo flying with no radio
contact and no navigation aids. It was an endurance test
with heavy turbulence but fair visibility until the buildup
in the early afternoon of the gigantic cumulonimbus storm
clouds.

With no radio navigation equipment in the aircraft I had
to rely entirely on map reading and dead-reckoning and the
use of such landmarks as rivers and the occasional railway

line. Although I had some anxious moments, I didn't manage to lose my way.

In the early stages of the flight, the parched brown savannah lands slowly gave way to the lush green of the tropical latitudes. Great Lake Victoria kept me company on my port side for hours and soothed my eyes after the harsh scrub of the savannah lands. After Kisumu in Kenya, the White Nile River guided me as it flowed through the Great Rift that divides the African continent. Gradually, the topography gave way again to the harshness of scrub that denotes the onset of the desert wastes. Midday temperatures reached the mid-forties, and after landing, the aircraft cabin turned into an oven. I kept a large thermos of lemon tea on the seat next to me with a tap from which I could drink while flying to make sure I would not become dehydrated. I had a large packet of dry biscuits and managed to exist for the five and a half days flying on this diet.

The Blue Nile and the White Nile meet in Khartoum and continue until the Mediterranean. In the final legs of the flight, the main problem was the turbulence, which was particularly severe in the heat of the African afternoons at comparatively low altitudes. I flew as early as possible in the mornings while it was still cool. Over the Sudan, the turbulence was so violent that my only course was to fly low and skim over the Nile at about twenty feet. That was my method right across the Sudan and Egypt, following the gentle turns of the river. I had to pull up when encountering the occasional tall-masted dhows with their lateen sails as they plied their way along the river. This kind of routing takes longer but was a welcome change from the endless beige-colored stretches of desert sand and made navigation much easier.

Without my auxiliary fuel tank, I had to stop at Luxor to spend the last night of the flight. I was unsure about landing and spending the night in what was about to be an enemy country, but I circled the field and landed. In response to Egyptian questions, I said I was on my way to England and would be heading out the next day for Beirut. I checked into one of the large hotels in Luxor. The hotel and city were full of British servicemen and servicewomen, all on short leave from their bases on the Suez Canal in Egypt.

The next day I hastened to fly the final leg to Palestine. Flight control at Luxor was polite, and their last words to me before take off after I filed the false flight plan for Beirut were, "The Jews in Palestine are causing trouble. Stay clear of them." I thanked them for their advice and replied that I would take care. I climbed to 8,000 feet and headed for the Gulf of Suez and the Sinai desert. After two hours in the glare of the desert wastes, the blue water of the Gulf of Suez appeared ahead of me. I began to feel that after the months of effort the long and exhausting flight would soon be bearing fruit with the arrival of the first reinforcement to our waning fleet.

With a feeling of homecoming, I crossed the southern Sinai desert and after a while saw far below in the brown distance a twinkling reflection of the harsh desert sun from a roof. It was one of the kibbutzim in the southern Negev, probably Kibbutz Gevulot. As the windscreen began to fill with the green of the cultivated fields and orchards in the northern Negev I saw Nir Am, the kibbutz to the east of

Gaza and the base of the southern detachment of our squadron at Sde Dov. I also anticipated being welcomed by Ezer, who was in charge of the Negev flight at the time of my departure.

I circled the kibbutz and landed on the narrow dirt strip, looking forward to the reunion with my companions whom I had left three months before. A group of kibbutzniks stood near my open cabin door. Instead of warm, welcoming faces, I met stony and suspicious expressions. I was shocked to note that some of them were holding weapons at the ready. Eli Eyal looked at me in astonishment and rushed forward to clasp me in a warm embrace. He asked me where I had come from and when I answered, "South Africa," there were incredulous looks from all around. I hastened to explain. They had watched the unknown silver-and-red aircraft approach from the direction of Egypt and circle the strip and thought that my aircraft was an enemy. Troops next to the runway had machine guns at the ready and were about to fire as I approached for landing. Fortunately, someone ordered to hold fire when it looked like I was about to land.

I was a target that could not have been missed approaching for a landing at low altitude and speed, and that would have been the end of me. So, after all the trials and tribulations involved in obtaining the aircraft and flying it all the way up Africa, the Bonanza and I were within an inch of ending our careers at the very moment of realizing our triumph. After refueling, I took off again and arrived at Sde Dov. Immediately after arriving, I was called to Hayarkon Street to headquarters to face a severe dressing down from

Premier Ben Gurion about the complaints from some members of the Jewish community in Johannesburg about my activities there. Unaware at that time of the desperate situation in Palestine, they thought that my insistence on declaring an emergency was unnecessary and that there was no reason for alarm.

Ben Gurion was a short, sturdy man with small, piercing dark eyes and a crop of white hair standing up high around his mostly bald pate. From his earliest youth in Poland, which he fled in 1906, he was devoted to Zionism and to socialism. He arrived as one of the early settlers in Palestine and became the leader of the powerful labor movement. He had an unusual diction in his Hebrew speech saying for instance *"avironum mivtsayum,"* instead of the more correct *"avironim mivtsaim."* He was called the "old man or "BG" by everyone, terms of endearment, for he was the most outstanding personality in the government both before and after the founding of the State of Israel. He was well aware of the details of my mission, and I must have fielded his criticisms satisfactorily, for that was the last complaint I had from him about the South African saga.

The three South African Fairchilds were flown from South Africa by volunteer pilots I had recruited and were escorted by a professional airline pilot and radio operator in the Rapide. They departed Johannesburg and made their way up the African continent in open formation, arriving in Cairo after two weeks. After leaving Cairo, they discovered they were being escorted by Egyptian Air Force Spitfires and had to change their routing. Instead of following the original plan of disappearing to Palestine after filing a flight plan for Benghazi in Libya, they had to fly to Italy. They eventually made it to Palestine. Though I had sent them off two weeks before I began my flight, they arrived a week after me. A second Rapide purchased in South Africa made its way two weeks after the first one, and on its arrival in Cairo, the Egyptians became suspicious, guessing that its destination was not London as declared. It was impounded. This same aircraft eventually arrived in Israel in 1951 when it was intercepted by Israel Air Force fighters over the Negev and forced to land at Beersheba—a somewhat roundabout journey from Johannesburg to Tel Aviv.

The first of the three Fairchilds to arrive was flown by a pilot who was unsure of the situation in Palestine and did not know what airfields were in our hands. Uncertain, he had arrived in the Jewish-held part; he was fortunate to have chosen Sde Dov. However, no sooner had he touched down than he heard shouts to take cover, and seconds later, there was a raid by Egyptian Air Force Spitfires. He was luckier than a group of American pilots shortly after who were ferrying two Norsemen planes from Europe and unwittingly landed in Egyptian-held El Arish, presenting them with one aircraft and four pilots, whom the Egyptians imprisoned.

THE BATTLE FOR JERUSALEM

While I was away in South Africa, heavy fighting began in Jerusalem. When it seemed the Old City would be unable to hold out against the attacks by the Arab Legion, the Harel brigade of the Palmach was transferred to Jerusalem. They penetrated the Jewish Quarter of the Old City through the Zion Gate in an attempt to save the city. But the situation was hopeless, and shortly afterward the people of the Old City were evacuated. While the fighting raged, a few hundred trucks managed to get through to Jerusalem from the coast. After the British left Palestine, the Arab Legion entered the fighting in earnest in the Old City and moved on to cut the road between Jerusalem and the coast at Bab el Wad (a steep pass with the mountains on both sides, the peaks held by the Arabs).

All road transport to Jerusalem must pass this defile. When the first convoy of the Haganah approached, the vehicles were fired on and stone barriers were laid on the road to block the passage of the convoys. The Haganah's armored cars led the attempts to go through the pass. The "armored cars" of the Haganah were homemade in various kibbutzim. Their armor was made of wooden boards sandwiched between steel sheets and afforded only minimal protection.

Located high above the road, the Arabs poured withering fire into the convoy causing heavy losses. Beit Mahsir was the largest Arab village on the heights and was the source of most of the continual shelling of the vehicles trying to maintain the precarious supply link between the coastal belt and Jerusalem.

The heavy fighting between Arab forces and the Harel Brigade concentrated mainly along Bab el Wad. The brigade made several attempts to capture the village but was repulsed time after time with heavy casualties. On 8 May, the

Newly winged Lt. Boris Senior, 1944. Although serving with an RAF squadron, he wears the uniform of his native South African Air Force (SAAF). *SAAF*

Leon Senior was six years older than Boris. A B-24 bomber commander with 31 Squadron, SAAF, he went missing in action a week before Boris's adventure off Venice. *SAAF*

A Kittyhawk IV of 250 Squadron, RAF. Essentially P-40Ns, these rugged Curtiss fighters flew ground-attack missions until the end of the war. *Author*

Members of 250 Squadron assemble around and on one of their "Kittys." Normally carrying two 500-pound bombs under their wings, these fighter-bombers could also tote a 1,000-pounder on their centerline fuselage stations. One of these large bombs serves as a point of interest in this group shot. The tall officer in light trousers and battledress jacket standing near the bomb is probably Maj. Felix Weingarten, a South African. *Andrew Thomas*

The USAAF took a number of Navy PBY Catalinas, redesignating them as OA-10s and using them as rescue aircraft in the Mediterranean theater. These views of the same aircraft, serial number 44-33939, shows the Cat before and after receiving a new paint job. *George W. Fox*

Views of 1st Emergency Rescue Squadron OA-10s over the
Mediterranean. *George W. Fox*

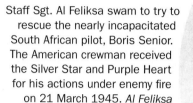

Staff Sgt. Al Feliksa swam to try to rescue the nearly incapacitated South African pilot, Boris Senior. The American crewman received the Silver Star and Purple Heart for his actions under enemy fire on 21 March 1945. *Al Feliksa*

The plane commander, Lt. Jack Dunn, receives the Air Medal for his role in the rescue. Brig. Gen. Charles Myers does the honors in May 1945. *Al Feliksa*

"Sam Bennet," Boris's undercover name while a member of the Irgun in 1947. He stands by an Auster liaison aircraft, one of the first types to enter service with the Sherut Avir, the predecessor of the Israel Air Force. *Author*

Now a colonel in the IAF in 1952, Boris wears his silver wings as well as a campaign ribbon for service in the War of Independence. *Author*

The Senior home in Johannesburg in 1941. *Author*

Having dinner near the *rondavel,* the circular thatched-roof building in the background, on the family farm. *Author*

The Seniors entertain Chaim Weizmann, co-founder and future first president of Israel in 1933. From left to right: Ethel Haynan, a member of the Zionist Movement; Boris's father, Woolf; Benzion Hersch, a lawyer; Mrs. Vera Weizmann; Chaim Weizmann; Mrs. Wolf, a friend; and Boris's mother, Annie. *Author*

Boris's parents stop in Africa en route to Palestine in 1939. The aircraft is probably an Imperial Airways Heracles, a biplane airliner of the day. *Author*

Prime Minister Yitzak Rabin (right) and Boris (left) enjoy the festivities at Boris's seventieth birthday in 1994. A year later, Rabin was assassinated by an Israeli dissident. *Author*

A de Havilland Tiger Moth of the Sherut Avir at Sde Dov airstrip north of Tel Aviv in early 1948. This particular aircraft, VQ-PAU, originally came from Canada. Other Moths and Taylorcraft light planes are in the background. *IAF*

A de Havilland Rapide taxis before a mission. Big and slow, these airliners flew a variety of peacetime and, occasionally, wartime missions. *IAF*

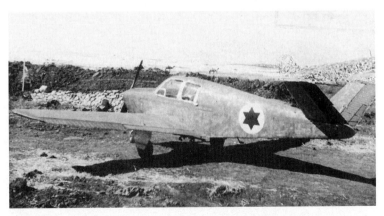

Boris Senior bought two Beechcraft Bonanzas and flew them on several bombing missions. The makeshift bomb racks can be seen just below the wings. Ultimately becoming a classic general-aviation design, the Bonanza saw its share of combat in 1948 flying for the Israelis. *IAF*

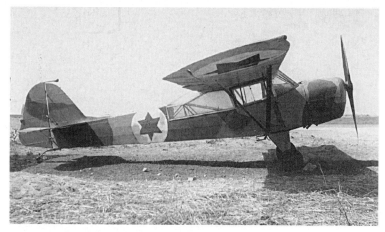

One of the main aircraft in the first days of the 1948 war was the British Auster AOP.3, often referred to as the Primus because the sound of its engine reminded many of its Israeli pilots of the kerosene stove by the same name. *IAF*

Piper Cubs have served long and well for more than fifty years with the IAF beginning in 1948 and ending as initiation trainers to give many students their first taste of flying. This is a PA-18-150 Super Cub. *IAF*

One of the oddest-looking types to serve in 1948 was the Miles Aerovan. It was lost in July 1948 when it crash-landed south of Tel Aviv and Arab irregulars attacked the crew, killing one. A few weeks before, Senior had flown the Aerovan to Jerusalem to evacuate women and children from the beleaguered city. *IAF*

Avia S-199s were Messerschmitts built in Czechoslovakia and powered with engines intended for Heinkel bombers. The result was an unforgiving aircraft that nonetheless provided Israel with its first fighter. Note the huge paddle-bladed propeller. *IAF*

Crewmen prepare for a mission beside one of three B-17 Flying Fortresses. The veteran bombers served through the 1956 Suez Campaign. *IAF*

D-120, an Avia fighter, taxis out to begin a mission. *IAF*

The few P-51 Mustangs obtained by the IAF represented one of the most-advanced types in service until the advent of jets. Senior scored one confirmed kill against the Egyptians in a P-51 and one in a Spitfire. *IAF*

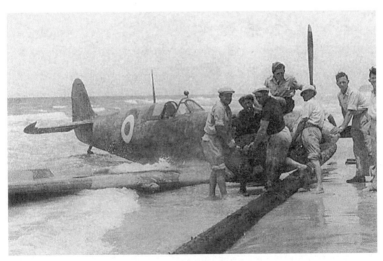

This Egyptian Spitfire was shot down on 15 May 1948. Its pilot crash-landed on a beach. *IAF*

Spitfires and their pathfinder C-54 on the airfield in Czechoslovakia before the start of Operation Velveta. Note the long-range fuel tanks beneath the Spitfires' wings. *Author*

Admittedly a poor photo, this nonetheless rare shot shows three Velveta Spitfires as seen from the cabin of the C-54. *Author*

commander of the brigade, Yitzhak Rabin, was ordered to capture Beit Mahsir at all cost. Mindful of the heavy casualties he had already suffered, he called for air support.

I had arrived just in time to offer help. At the time I landed in the Bonanza from South Africa, the desperate shortage of aircraft and pilots made it impossible for me to check out anyone else on the Bonanza, so I had to fly urgent missions to Bab el Wad day and night. My precious Bonanza, still with the African dust on its undercarriage, entered the fray the day I arrived in Israel. We put up a small tent near the runway in Sde Dov where, utterly exhausted, I rested between the night flights.

I logged sixty night hours in the blackout with minimal instruments in ten days. My job in the Bonanza, apart from the occasional bomb thrown out through the luggage door, was to carry an army signaler with a large World War II walkie-talkie between his legs with the antenna protruding through the hole in the perspex canopy. His duty was to communicate with the ground troops.

On one occasion when I was flying low over the Arab positions in Beit Mahsir, a bullet passed through the belly of the Bonanza and smashed the plastic tail trim wheel between my knees. I had to land without a trim wheel.

A former Russian Air Force technician fitted my Bonanza with electrically operated bomb racks under the wings. This made for better accuracy for dive-bombing. I made sure to seek him out and congratulate him on his achievement. However, my trust in his technical abilities did not extend to allowing him to install a synchronized machine gun that could fire through the propeller, which he begged me to let him do.

After bombing the village a number of times with the Bonanza using 50-kilo Double Pushkins, I saw that, apart from keeping the enemy's heads down during the bombing and having some effect on their morale, we were not accomplishing much. I suggested to headquarters that something be done to drop heavier bombs, especially just before our ground forces attacked. The losses our Palmach troops had suffered were unsustainable, and the impossibility of keeping Jerusalem supplied while the Arab forces in Beit Mahsir held on to their positions overlooking the pass made it imperative to somehow give better support from the air.

One of our two Norduyn Norsemen was pressed into service. By then, we had some experience in making bombs and we filled a 200-liter drum with dynamite with a fuse on the lid. The fuse had to be lit before throwing it out of the aircraft. Our expert in bomb-making was a former RAF engineer, and he planned and supervised the making of our bombs at that time. When I suggested he accompany me on flights to test his bombs, he refused and that should have kindled my suspicion. On 10 May 1948 a large new drum bomb was lifted into a Norseman and a crew of four in addition to the two pilots climbed into the machine. They made several attempts to reach Beit Mahsir but without success because of low cloud cover and returned to base. In the meantime, I managed to keep up my bombing missions in the Bonanza.

Later that morning while I was in the air on the same mission for the second time, the Norseman again took off with a crew of six. The pilot in command was Yariv Shein-baum, the flying controller who received me at the steps of the aircraft on my first arrival in Palestine some months before. They climbed to 6,000 feet in the direction of the Jerusalem hills toward Beit Mahsir and reported that they were diving toward the target. I was already struggling with the bad visibility, but I found a hole in the cloud and dived through to drop my bombs on Beit Mahsir. The Norseman failed to return, and after some days we heard that witnesses had seen the Norseman diving through the cloud into a hill with a tremendous explosion.

There have been various theories about what happened, including an army report, which maintained they were shot down by an RAF Spitfire. My own theory is that when they moved the heavy barrel-bomb to the back of the aircraft ready for pushing out through the rear door, they upset the aircraft's center of gravity and went into an uncontrollable spin. There were reports that a British Spitfire was seen in the area at the time they crashed, but quite probably, the observers confused my Bonanza, which was new and un-known to anyone at the time, with a Spitfire.

Our reporting system was bad, and evidently no one told Yariv's young wife because no one knew for some time about the eyewitness reports confirming the crash. For some days after his disappearance, his wife Aya appeared every lunch time at Café Kassit, where the aircrews gathered asking if anyone knew where Yariv was. Each one of us left hurriedly when we saw her approaching.

Though of vital importance, strategically Jerusalem was no less important from an emotional standpoint, having been the focus of all Jewish hopes and dreams since the conquest and the destruction of the Temple by the Romans 2,000 years before. It had no airfield, and our forces cleared a short strip some 500 meters long in the Valley of the Cross, so called because tradition has it that a small forest was there and the cross on which Jesus was crucified was cut from it.

At the end of the strip was a fortress-like monastery built in the Middle Ages. It was a stone building with a high defensive wall surrounding it erected for protection against intruders or invading troops. This made it necessary for me to open to full throttle while keeping my feet on the brakes, and then releasing them immediately before takeoff to get over the wall. It was essential to gather maximum speed on the short takeoff run and to pull the stick back just before reaching the wall almost at stalling speed. After accomplishing that part of the flight, further speed was gained by flying down a conveniently located wadi. Only then could one gain sufficient height to climb over the mountains between Jerusalem and the coast.

This was hard enough in one of the smaller aircraft, but I tried to land a much larger aircraft, the twin-engine Aerovan capable of carrying nine passengers. With its two Gipsy Major engines, it was underpowered, and taking it into Jerusalem was a risky affair. The only approach to the field meant flying a tight circuit over the western edge of the city and then diving steeply to the landing. This did not always prevent us from being shot at by the Arab forces in East Jerusalem during the landing approach. This large airplane had not been seen before in Jerusalem, and when I first landed, crowds of Jerusalemites came to the strip to look at it.

Jerusalem was now under siege, cut off from the rest of the country with only an occasional convoy managing to get through. To this day wrecked armored cars can be seen as memorials on the sides of the main road near Bab el Wad.

The shortage of food and other commodities in Jerusalem was serious and could be seen in the pale wan faces of the crowd at the airstrip. Often, people appeared at Sde Dov airfield before I took off for Jerusalem with homemade cakes and biscuits, begging me to take them to their loved ones in the besieged city.

On my second flight to Jerusalem in the Aerovan to evacuate women and children, there were two incidents, one nearly fatal. Just before taking off from Jerusalem, and purely by chance, I discovered two air mechanics from a base near Tel Aviv stowed away in the space behind the rear seat. Had I not discovered them, we would certainly not have made it, for we were loaded to the hilt without them and with their additional weight would have crashed into the monastery. They were not prosecuted or court-martialed as laws and regulations were not enforced efficiently in Israel at that time.

After taking off and passing over the Trappist monastery at Latrun, which lies between the mountains of Jerusalem and the coast, my port engine failed. I feathered the propeller and, though losing height, reached the field at Sde Dov on one engine. The same Aerovan came to a tragic end three months later while on a flight back from the Dead Sea with men and women who were being evacuated. It made a forced landing on the beach twenty-five kilometers south of Tel Aviv and was surrounded by Arab guerrillas, who butchered the occupants. Three survived. One of them played dead and two went for help. The fourth occupant was killed.

MEDAL FOR A SABRA

Sdom was a strategically important location for us at the southern tip of the Dead Sea. It was cut off from the rest of Israel soon after hostilities began. As we couldn't fly there during daylight because of the danger of being shot down by enemy fighters, we had to fly there only by night. In the blackout that was no easy task, for the Dead Sea is more than a thousand feet below sea level. There were no navigational aids so we had to use the minimal instruments of the aircraft as well as fly by the seat of our pants. It meant reaching Beersheba, which was identified by the few roads converging on the darkened city. From there we had to turn left to the southeast and search for the glimmer of the Dead Sea.

We kept a close watch on the altimeter, for it was an uneasy experience to be letting down in the darkness without navigational aids. The mountains in nearby Hebron are more than a thousand feet above sea level, and with Sdom a thousand feet below, it was eerie to continue descending after the altimeter needle hit the bottom of the scale. With no lights we felt as if we were descending into the bowels of the earth.

At last we would see the runway flares being lighted. With no radio contact, the only way for them to know when we were arriving was by the sound of our engines, after which they hurriedly kindled the paraffin landing flares. Besides the disorientation caused by descending well below sea level without being able to know the height from the altimeter, the mountains to the east and west of Sdom presented a further hazard in the darkness. The only safe approach and departure from the strip was from over the water or down the Arava Valley.

Many of the missions were to evacuate seriously wounded kibbutzniks and servicemen, and these flights in particular gave me satisfaction. I remember well one such flight. One afternoon in May 1948, I was in my office in the long wooden hut at Sde Dov awaiting nightfall. The pilots not on duty were making their way to lodgings in Tel Aviv, and paraffin gooseneck flares were being laid out for night flights. The telephone rang; GHQ was on the line. A young kibbutznik in the children's settlement of Ben Shemen was seriously wounded during an attack by Arab irregular forces. The only way to save his life would be to get him quickly to a hospital. Ben Shemen is a kibbutz that housed mainly children who had escaped from the areas under Hitler and was famous for its excellence in education. It was cut off in the early stages of the war by the Arab guerrillas from Ramleh and Lydda.

Not overjoyed at the prospect of flying in and out of an unlighted, hardly marked strip at dusk under fire, I took off from Sde Dov in the waning light. Ben Shemen is near the Arab town of Hadita and a very tight circuit was called for.

This time the Arab forces were waiting with heavy small-arms fire. After I landed, a barely conscious boy was laid in the back of the Bonanza on the floor. During the short flight back to Tel Aviv, I tried to comfort him but he died during the flight. I was alone in the night with the dead boy. I landed at Sde Dov and the body was removed. A harrowing experience.

Ben Shemen was the scene of a heroic action by one of the young Palmach pilots, Zvi Ziebel, known to all of us as "Chibbie." On one flight to Ben Shemen, there was heavy firing from nearby Hadita. The firing was so intense that the aircraft was in danger even while on the ground. Chibbie got hold of a tractor, and after loading it with sacks of sand, placed it between the Auster and the direction from which the firing came. When he was ready for takeoff, he taxied the Auster slowly to the upwind end of the strip with a kibbutznik keeping the tractor between himself and the firing and took off without being hit. Chibbie survived for most of the war but was eventually shot down in his defenseless Auster by a flight of four Egyptian Spitfires.

When a committee was set up toward the end of the war to decide on the award of the first medals to be granted to our troops, I was appointed as the air force representative. In recognition of the bravery of the young Sabra pilots, I recommended that the coveted Medal of Valor be granted posthumously to Chibbie, and he became the only member of the air force to be awarded this highest decoration. In retrospect I believe it was a mistake not to have recommended an award to at least one of the non-Israeli volunteer pilots, the Mahalniks, who did the bulk of the fighting in the air. [MAHAL was an acronym from the Hebrew *Mit-nadvey huts la'aretz,* meaning "volunteers from outside the country."—ed.]

After the end of the mandate in May 1948, we gradually moved from a purely defensive role to one of active support in bombing, and our function became critically important. Army headquarters began to call urgently for our help.

The attacks by Arabs increased daily, and Haganah headquarters sought ways to get intelligence data not only about forthcoming attacks but also about the masses of neighboring Arabs pouring into Palestine from all sides to assist their brethren in the war. The nascent Air Service carried out many flights for reconnaissance and photography. We flew lower than ten or twenty feet above the ground carrying Leica cameras held in our hands while flying the aircraft. We often ran into heavy small-arms fire and were such easy targets it is miraculous no one was brought down.

The shortage of equipment and trained personnel was so critical that preventable accidents occurred. An example was the case of what happened to one of the South African Mahalniks. One morning early in June in my sleep, I heard a huge explosion from the direction of Sde Dov. I rushed down to the field and saw a column of smoke rising from a taxi track near the runway. One of our Fairchilds was burning near a large hole in the tarmac.

Evidently, a sleepy corpsman had walked into the spinning propeller carrying a 50-kilo bomb, which exploded. There was nothing left of him apart from burned pieces of flesh scattered around the tarmac. The South African volunteer pilot, Lionel Kaplan (Kappy) was sitting in the cock-

pit and saw what was going to happen. He tried to get out
in time. Kappy was injured by the explosion; the next time
I saw him was in a hospital bed with one eye missing and
many shrapnel wounds in his face. When he recovered he
tried to continue flying with his glass eye and made a few
flights before he was permanently grounded.

In many cases we were unable to fly the missions GHQ
called for, desperate to help hard-pressed forces in the isolated settlements. They had no experience in the handling
of an air arm and had little idea of what was and was not
possible with an airplane. Moreover, I am certain that no
air force has ever had to fly the missions we carried out with
the inadequate equipment and inexperienced pilots at our
disposal.

There is no doubt that in the War of Independence, especially during the first half of 1948, the aircraft that arrived
from South Africa played a crucial role in the survival of
Israel. The thirteen aircraft purchased and flown from Johannesburg to Palestine with their volunteer crews more
than tripled the strength of the Air Service at that critical
time. Later, the stream of airplanes and crews from the
United States and Europe provided more suitable and more
effective tools necessary to fight and finish Israel's first and
most crucial war.

CHAPTER SEVEN

Independence

FINAL STEPS

O N 15 May 1948, the unofficial war became a full-fledged open conflict. The tension reached breaking point as the Yishuv feverishly prepared to face the onslaught of the invading Arab armies. The scale of the simultaneous attack by the invading forces of six nations on five fronts is not generally appreciated. They looked as though they would quickly overwhelm Israel. It should be of some interest to students of military history to determine how it was that Israel not only survived the onslaught, but within a year was victorious. If the populations of the attacking countries are brought into the equation, the figures are astonishing. Ranged against the half a million Jewish residents of the Yishuv were more than 40 million Arabs, supported by Muslim communities throughout the world.

If the coming generations in Israel have any doubt of the heroism of their forebears, let them learn the details of Israel's history of 1948 and 1949, of Kfar Etzion, Kfar Darom,

Zemach, and other settlements that stood against impossible odds. They will then be encouraged in times of adversity.

At the beginning of May 1948, the military chiefs of the Arab League met in Damascus to plan the invasion and subsequent division of Palestine into areas to be occupied by their respective countries. The war plans of the Arab countries were comprehensive, a full-scale invasion supported by air and naval forces.

In the north, the Lebanese were to advance along the coast north of Haifa to Nahariya. In the east, the Syrians would head for Galilee in a two-pronged attack on the northern end of the Sea of Galilee and on the southern end. The Iraqis planned to attack from the east to Natanya on the coast in an attempt to cut Israel into two at its narrow waistline. In the east, a brigade of the Arab Legion would advance on Tel Aviv. On 19 May, Azzam Pasha of the Arab League said each invading force would establish its own administration in the area it would shortly be conquering.

A few days before the final evacuation of the British, Golda Meir, a minister in the Israeli government, disguised herself as an Arab and secretly met King Abdullah of Transjordan to try to dissuade him from taking part in the invasion of Palestine. Her mission failed. The British-officered Arab Legion invaded Palestine together with the other Arab armies.

In the south, the Egyptians planned to advance in two columns with the main attack coming from El Arish and advancing along the coast via Gaza to Tel Aviv. A second force would head for the southern flank of Jerusalem through Beersheba and Hebron to link up with the Arab Legion forces of Transjordan. Arab irregular forces of the Moslem Brotherhood inside Palestine were to support the invading armies.

Facing these assaults were the irregular troops of the former Israeli underground fighters who had for years had difficulties in illegally stockpiling their light weapons in bunkers. They had to conceal them from the British forces of the mandatory regime. In the air, Israel had only the few light aircraft acquired in circumstances already described.

After the invasion began, the flight of a major part of the Arab population from Palestine in 1948 gave birth to a human tragedy that remains with us to this day. The reasons for the wholesale exodus are complex but must in no small measure be attributed to the propaganda beamed to them from the neighboring Arab countries. They urged the refugees to leave for what was to be a temporary absence until the "Jews had been driven into the sea by the invading Arab armies," to quote the Mufti of Jerusalem. They were told to vacate the battle zones so as not to impede the free movement of the invading troops. The deceptive horror stories about what the Jews would do to them was also a major factor. The wealthier families led the exodus to neighboring countries.

There were many cases of Jewish institutions in Israel appealing on the radio and in the press to the Arab residents not to leave. The advice was ignored and a mass exodus ensued. It is on record, for example, that the British superintendent of police in Haifa reported, "The Jews were making every effort to persuade the Arab populace to stay."

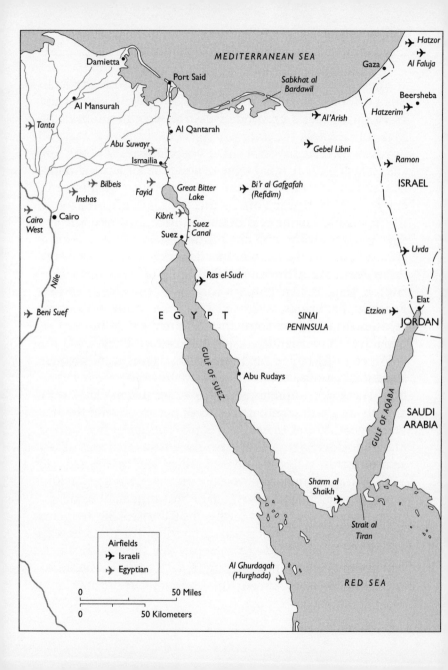

Though I was unaware of the details of the Arab preparations for war, I knew 15 May was to be a fateful day for us. I flew out to make a reconnaissance on the afternoon of 14 May. I flew along the proposed borders of the new State of Israel as defined by the United Nations partition plan of December 1947. It was a time of much disorder; the flight was initiated by neither the air force headquarters nor general headquarters. That is not surprising because there were no established chains of command at that time.

I took off for the reconnaissance in the Bonanza with a crew of two to take photographs and note what we saw on the ground. We made for the Bnot Ya'acov Bridge over the river Jordan, the main approach from Syria to Palestine. Reaching the bridge, I was shocked to see a line of military vehicles stretching as far as the eye could see from deep in Syria over the Jordan River and into eastern Palestine.

We counted large numbers of army vehicles, all painted in dark green camouflage and heading in convoy into Palestine. There were more than 2,000 trucks, armored cars with ambulances, tanks, and artillery transporters. A similar picture repeated itself when we flew to the Allenby Bridge, the main approach over the Jordan River from Transjordan to Jerusalem.

Knowing the rag-tail units of our citizen army using lorries, vans, and buses collected from commercial businesses often with the advertisements still on their sides, we were distraught to see below us large, organized army formations advancing in military order into Palestine. For the first and perhaps only time since arriving in the country, I began to fear for the coming day. Many of these foreign army units were well inside the Palestine borders before the British pulled out.

During the flight we passed near the RAF base of Mafrak in Transjordan. It was not far from the border, and as we flew near on our reconnaissance, I saw a fighter taking off. Fearing that it was an RAF Spitfire I turned west toward home. Fortunately, we were not of enough interest to warrant examination by the British fighter.

Immediately after landing at Sde Dov, I reported to deputy chief of staff Yigael Yadin at GHQ. When I blurted out what I thought was my bombshell, he laconically replied, "Yes, we know all about it," showing no emotion.

Yadin's opinions carried much weight for he was a fine soldier, had held highly responsible positions in the unofficial military hierarchy, and I had complete confidence in him. In civilian life he was a highly respected archaeologist. He was actively involved in the defense sector from early 1947 after being appointed chief of operations of the Haganah. In the War of Independence, he acted as deputy chief of staff under General Dori and later after the end of the war in 1949 was appointed chief of staff of the Israel Defense Force. In May 1977 he became deputy prime minister to Menachem Begin.

Despite my confidence in him and expecting a land and air attack any moment, I was not reassured by his reaction to my news. I insisted that we disperse our aircraft from Sde Dov to the three satellite strips we had prepared in Herzlia, Even Yehuda, and Kibbutz Shfayim. All three strips were a short distance from Tel Aviv and could have been operational in a matter of days. Reluctantly, I accepted Yadin's order that the aircraft stay at Sde Dov.

My relations with Yadin were cordial, and I had been able to advise him regarding air operations for a considerable time. Most regretfully on this occasion, he did not accept my advice and the damage caused to our small fleet by the Egyptian air raids the following morning seriously affected our strength in the air. Yadin's attitude reflected the prevailing ignorance of air force matters on the part of the Palmach and the Haganah. This view lasted for many months until the air force got its rightful priorities from the government in late 1948.

The Iraqi Air Force had a number of modern British fighter aircraft, but the Egyptian Air Force was equipped with large numbers of modern fighters and bombers and was the major threat to Israel. Admittedly, its aircrews didn't have anything like the battle experience of our volunteer fighter pilots who were to arrive before long, but they were an infinitely superior force compared to the few weekend pilots and toy planes of the Israel Air Force at that time. The British army general staff headed by Field Marshal Montgomery reported to the British government, "When Britain evacuates Palestine, the Jews will immediately be overcome."

The inevitability of war cast a pall on the elation of the Jews waiting eagerly for the founding of the infant state at midnight on 14 May 1948. In the early evening of 14 May, Ben Gurion as prime minister designate speaking in the name of the National Council of the Yishuv, extended a hand of peace to the Arabs of Palestine and to the neighboring countries, and invited them to cooperate with the independent Jewish nation for the good of all. These overtures were ignored, and the fully equipped regular armed forces of Egypt, Transjordan, Syria, Lebanon, and Iraq, with units of the Saudi Arabian army in support, invaded Palestine the next day. Ben Gurion announced that the name of the new nation state would be Israel and that it would immediately be open for unrestricted Jewish immigration, for the "ingathering of the exiles."

The rejoicing of the Jews at their new statehood, which they regained after 2,000 years, was tempered by the difficulties resulting mainly from the plight of the kibbutz settlements. The British controlled all transport arteries, ports, and airports. The borders with Transjordan and Egypt were policed largely by Arab troops and served as convenient channels for the passage into Palestine of Arab forces and arms. Apart from the few large population centers of Tel Aviv, Jerusalem, and Haifa, the kibbutzim were spread mainly in the Plain of Jezreel and on the coastal plain bordering the Mediterranean. Some settlements, particularly those in the Negev in the south of the country, were particularly vulnerable.

Communication between the kibbutzim and the rest of Israel was a major problem. Well aware of this the Arabs concentrated their attacks initially on these soft targets. The Air Service was to play a vital role in providing supplies to the settlements surrounded and cut off from the main body of the Yishuv.

For months before the UN resolution on partition in November 1947, the Palestinian Jews had begun to organize themselves into military formations. They had the Haganah with its Palmach shock troops approximately 3,000 strong and the very much smaller urban forces of the Irgun based mainly in the cities and opposing the British military forces in Palestine and abroad. There was little military equipment, and what they did possess had been collected from the world's scrap heaps usually lacking spare parts and manuals of operation. Language was also a problem, for there must have been a dozen languages spoken in the Yishuv (Jewish-settled areas of the country), including Hebrew and English. In the air force, most of the flying personnel knew only English, whereas the support people, such as tower operators, spoke Hebrew exclusively.

The Jews, however, had a powerful weapon—what is known in Hebrew as *Ain brera*, meaning "no alternative." In other words, the Jews were fighting for their survival with their backs to the wall, or rather the sea. Losing the war would have meant in the best case losing their homeland, and in the worst case their lives. For many it meant a return to persecution. Each and every battle was fought on a background of desperation knowing the fate that faced them if a single battle was lost. The memory of the Holocaust just three years before cast an ever-present shadow on the Jewish fighters and accounts, in part, for the desperate heroism shown by the fighting men and women of Israel.

On 14 May the British flag was lowered for the last time in Palestine. That was the signal for the mass invasion by the Arabs. The Egyptian forces split into two formations, one of which began its advance on Tel Aviv via the coastal road while the other captured Auja on the Egyptian-Palestine border near Kibbutz Revivim. They then headed toward Beersheba and Hebron with the intention of linking up with the Transjordanian forces to the south of Jerusalem. In the meantime, the Transjordanians had crossed the Jordan River at the Allenby Bridge and made for Latrun in the coastal plain, some thirty kilometers from Tel Aviv. They reached Latrun two days after the State of Israel was declared.

While I was in the air on the reconnaissance flight around the northern and eastern borders of Palestine, a crucial drama was being enacted below us. Even before the formal ending of the mandate, Arab troops were advancing into the country. On the final day of the British mandate, units of the Arab Legion tried capturing the strategic police post at Gesher. After failing to overcome the resistance of the settlers, they diverted their forces and occupied the hydroelectric power station at Naharayim on the Jordan River.

The Iraqi army tried to cross the Jordan River at Gesher, but when they encountered ferocious resistance from the settlers of the Golani Brigade, they abandoned the crossing. In the meantime, the Syrian army began heavy artillery bombardments on the kibbutzim south of the Sea of Galilee and, in particular, on Kibbutz Ein Gev on the eastern shore of the lake. Again, a single battalion of the Golani Brigade was left on its own to defend the entire area against invasion by the armies of two sovereign states.

Israeli soldiers, who were holding positions in the Arab town of Zemach, couldn't withstand the attacks of the armored cars and tanks of the Syrians. On 18 May the kibbutz fell to the invaders after trying to defend themselves with

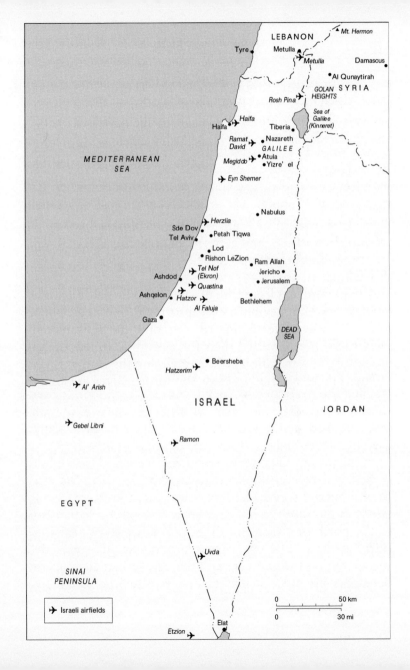

two 20mm anti-aircraft guns. By 20 May, the defenders had been wiped out almost to a man, and the way was open for the Syrian armor to advance to the settlement of Degania. More fierce battles ensued with the outnumbered and poorly armed settlers fighting for their lives and families. Eventually it ended in defeat for the Syrian forces, which withdrew from the area and diverted their attacks to the north near Mishmar Hayarden. The successful defense against the superior forces at Degania, known in Israel as "the Mother of the Settlements," gave a huge boost to morale in Israel at a time when it was battling for its very existence.

The Lebanese army invaded Galilee from the north and overcame the settlements of Kadesh and Naftali. Within a day, however, the Israeli settlers recaptured them from the Lebanese together with a large number of weapons. On the central front, the Iraqi army transferred the brunt of its attack to the south of the Sea of Galilee, and by 25 May had reached the Arab town of Nablus not far from the Mediterranean coast. The advance of their forward units was stopped only ten kilometers from the city of Natanya thereby preventing the threat to cut Israel into two.

In the Jordan Valley, the Arab Legion entered the kibbutz of Beit Ha'arava at the northern end of the Dead Sea after the kibbutzniks evacuated the settlement and escaped to Sdom in the south in boats. After capturing the settlements to the north of Jerusalem, the legion advanced to the outskirts of the capital city. Heavy artillery shelling preceded the attacks on the Old City and the new Jewish city, but the defenders put up a fierce resistance. After the legion had suffered heavy losses, their British commander, Glubb Pasha, called off the attack. This was fortunate for the legion was by then only a few hundred meters from the center of the Jewish-held part of the city. The legion attacks were not limited to the northern sector of the city, and in the south battles led to the fall and subsequent recapture of Kibbutz Ramat Rachel where the Transjordanians were supported by the armed forces of their Egyptian allies. The battle was then concentrated on the Old City, and despite furious fighting by the Palmach units, the Old City fell to the legion.

FIRST EGYPTIAN AIR RAID

The war in the air had begun inauspiciously for us in the air force. On the morning of 15 May 1948, the day the British mandate ended and the State of Israel was born, I was asleep in the Yarden Hotel in Tel Aviv after the long reconnaissance along the borders the day before. At 0525 that morning, I awoke to sounds I knew well, the unmistakable roar of Rolls-Royce Merlin engines, the sound of bomb blasts, and the rat-tat-tat of machine guns. I rushed downstairs and saw pilots bursting into the foyer, some of them with their wives in nightdresses, distraught and bewildered.

There was a jeep outside the hotel, and I jumped into it and drove furiously to Sde Dov. The scene shook me. Two waves of Egyptian Spitfires had already plastered the field, badly damaging our fleet of aircraft. Against my advice, headquarters had arranged the entire fleet in neatly parked rows on either side of the runway.

The Bonanza, which had cost me so much effort to fly from Africa only ten days before, was parked on the north side of the runway severely damaged by a bomb. I was livid at GHQ's stupidity in leaving the aircraft on the field despite my pleas. A number of other aircraft were badly damaged by the attacking Spitfires.

There was a large gaping hole in the wall of our only hangar, and an angry fire raged in the green hut that housed the armory. Near it stood one of the ground crew wailing uncontrollably that his friend, one of the corpsmen, was trapped inside the hut.

Because of the embargo imposed by the United States and Britain on weapons and planes, Israel's purchasing efforts had been badly hindered. We were virtually without aircraft to face the Arab fighters and bombers, who had been buying freely whatever they wanted for years before the war. After the bombing we were left with virtually no serviceable aircraft.

At the start of the War of Independence on 15 May 1948, the small group of exhausted pilots with their battered airplanes was on the verge of collapse. A statement made on 12 May by Yigael Yadin to the Provisional Council of the Government testified to the gravity of the situation at that time. "We have no air force. Our planes operate contrary to all the rules of aerial tactics. We have already had grievous losses. No other pilots would dare to take off in planes like ours. . . . The Arab air forces are a hundred and fifty times the size of ours. It would be best not to take into account the planes we have as a military factor."

While I was observing the sorry scene at Sde Dov, we

heard the whine of the Merlins again and ran to take cover in a nearby field. We had made no preparations in case of a bombing, neither shelters nor foxholes. The field was the site of a small cement factory and the piles of blocks drying in the sun gave us cover from the strafing fighters. I glanced around me and saw someone lying nearby dressed in a tweed jacket, khaki shorts, and long socks like a British soldier or policeman. It was Chief of Staff Yigael Yadin.

As the whine of the Spitfires faded away, a large black car drove gingerly over the wooden bridge at the edge of the airfield and out stepped Prime Minister Ben Gurion. He carried a pair of large black binoculars, which he promptly trained on the scene. I was enraged at the equanimity with which my warning had been received and with the outcome plainly to be seen in front of us. Without realizing what I was doing, I started shouting at Ben Gurion, cursing the GHQ and roaring, "I warned them and now look at this. What idiocy!" Ben Gurion looked at me in surprise and without saying a word got into his car and disappeared over the bridge just in time to miss the third wave of Spitfires. In a mindless rage, I pulled out my revolver and though the attacking Spitfires could see me clearly in front and below their noses during the dive, futilely shot at the fighters as they roared past at the bottom of their dives.

In charge of the few anti-aircraft guns was a man slightly older than us, whom I had not seen before at the field. When the raid started, he began to scream orders to his men in a hysterical tone of voice. I went up to him and silenced him, because I could see that his behavior was affecting everyone around him. He drew himself up in a show of exaggerated importance and said to me, "Do you know who I am?"

I replied, "I don't know and I don't care, but do you know who I am? I am the commander of this base, and I tell you to shut up. You are causing panic."

A fourth raid that morning followed shortly with more damage to our fleet. During the raid I saw a telltale stream of Glycol coolant pouring from one of the attacking Spitfires, a clear sign it had been hit and would have to crashland. It had been hit by one of the 20mm anti-aircraft guns placed at three points around the airfield. I watched the Egyptian aircraft lose height as it headed away from the field to the north.

After checking that more Egyptian fighters were not about to appear, I took off hurriedly in the remaining Bonanza in the direction of the Spit. It had force-landed on Herzlia beach fifteen kilometers north of Sde Dov. Apart from one wing, which had been torn off during the landing, it looked as though the pilot should have gotten out all right. After circling it once, I landed on a satellite strip on what is now Rehov Shalvah in the suburb of Herzlia Pituah, drew my pistol, and ran toward the beach. On the way I was stopped by a soldier in a command car, who told me the pilot was in our hands. He drove me to where he was being held.

In an abandoned factory near the seafront, I found the Egyptian pilot nursing a wound on the back of his head, obviously in a state of shock and fear. Realizing his mental state, I somewhat pompously said to him in English, "You have no need to fear. You will be treated according to the

Geneva Convention," though I had no idea of the exact provisions of the convention. I asked him how he got the wound on the back of his head, for when crashing an aircraft one gets hurt in the front of the head. He replied, "I landed all right, but when I tried to get out of the aircraft, a soldier came up and hit me on the back of my head with a Sten gun."

After making sure that he was not badly injured, I blindfolded him and flew him to Sde Dov, from which I took him to Tel Aviv for interrogation. The commander of the air force, Aharon Remez, and Dan Tolkowski, chief of operations, joined me in the interrogation. The Egyptian was Flight Lieutenant Baraka. He was forthcoming in his replies to our questions, maintaining that the Egyptian air force had sixty Spitfires, of which, about forty were serviceable. Aware of our total lack of any military aircraft, this information shocked us.

Baraka kept muttering, "You Israelis have very good wireless," which I eventually understood to mean that we had good intelligence services. Throughout the interrogation he was unusually nervous and depressed. He asked me for permission to go to the toilet. I took him to the bathroom, asking a guard with a Sten gun to accompany us. When Baraka saw the guard, he became very agitated and said, "Please sir do not kill me now." I calmed him down, and after that, he continued to answer our questions.

He was married with two children and had at one time been employed at the Egyptian air ministry. He was later transferred to a prison camp and after the war returned to

Egypt in a subsequent exchange of prisoners, but minus his wings, which I removed from his uniform as a souvenir.

Even allowing for the effect on him of crash-landing his aircraft in enemy territory and suddenly ending up as a prisoner of war, I thought that he seemed not only stunned but unusually terrified. He was evidently not well briefed, for he could probably have glided with his dead engine from Sde Dov to Lydda Airport, which was in the hands of his Transjordanian allies, saving his aircraft and himself from imprisonment in Israel for the duration of the war.

In the bombing of the airfield at Sde Dov early in the morning of 15 May and four times thereafter on the same day, our twin-engine Rapide was destroyed, one Bonanza was badly damaged, as were the RWD 13 and two Austers. Although other aircraft at the field suffered less damage, we were largely grounded. We had lost five men killed and nine wounded.

Baraka was not the only prisoner of war with whom I had contact. A second Egyptian Spitfire was shot down by an RAF fighter not long after Baraka. This was after an attack by Egyptian Air Force Spitfires on the RAF base at Ramat David near Haifa. This base remained in British hands for a few days after the expiration of the mandate, covering the British exodus. It was faulty intelligence on the part of the Egyptians for presuming it to be an Israel Air Force base.

Britain had powerful air force units in the Middle East at the time. After the first bombing of Ramat David, the Egyptian Air Force returned for another raid, but the RAF had a Spitfire patrol in the air over the field when the Egyptians came in for a second attack. Without too much trouble, the

RAF fighters shot one down and the pilot, Flight Lieutenant Eynan, baled out. He landed near Kibbutz Dalia in the Carmel range and was taken prisoner by Israeli forces. Unbelievably, the Egyptian Spitfires later returned for a third attack. In total they lost five Spits in that one day. When Eynan was shot down, the news came to Israel Air Force headquarters in Tel Aviv where I was at the time deputy chief of operations.

I immediately drove to Dalia and found the Egyptian pilot sitting in a storeroom. He was a hairy, thickset man dressed in an undershirt, but he did not seem as deeply dejected as his predecessor Baraka. I took him blindfolded in my car to air force headquarters in Tel Aviv and used the time during the journey of some two hours to interrogate him. He told me he had done training on Harvards and readily answered questions. When I asked him what the stalling speed of the Harvard was, he replied, "Sixty-nine miles per hour."

I gently said, "No, it is sixty-seven." He immediately clammed up and refused to answer another question. I had flown seventy-five hours in the Harvard during training.

After the first bombing, we were unable to do much flying. When we did get airborne, we were fired on by our own troops for they had no way of identifying us as friend or foe. There was an urgent need to have easily recognizable markings on our aircraft. I got someone to paint a Magen David (Star of David) on the fuselage and wings of one of the Austers and had one of the pilots fly the aircraft around the circuit. None of us could make out the marking from the ground, so I told the painter to fill in the Star of David in a solid, dark blue color and to paint a white circle around it. A few circuits at up to a thousand feet proved that the markings were now clearly visible, and I gave instructions to paint the rest of the aircraft. To this day the Israel Air Force uses these markings, and they are a constant reminder to me of the dark old days when our backs were to the wall. Since then aircraft so emblazoned have flown great missions as far as Iraq in the north and across the Mediterranean to Tunis in the west.

Aharon Remez, a young Sabra with a deep commitment to the Zionist dream of a Jewish state, was eventually appointed as the head of the air force. His father was a close associate of Prime Minister Ben Gurion and one of the stalwarts of the Histadrut general trade union, which was the dominant power in Israel for years before and after the founding of the state. Remez had shortly before been released as a pilot from the RAF and had gone to the United States for a year to study. Though only having been a sergeant pilot, he had a comprehensive understanding of the role of an air force. He carried on a running fight with general headquarters, which had no experience in air warfare and tended to treat the air force more or less like another battalion that operated in a different medium, the air. This conflict led to endless friction between general headquarters and air force headquarters

Remez fought for a larger measure of independence and an increased budget for the air force. Throughout the war I saw him returning day after day exhausted from long tussles with the general staff on the subject. He did not succeed completely in his fight but did achieve a certain measure of operational independence for the air force. He stayed in command throughout the War of Independence and did an excellent job during a period crucial for the nascent air force and the State of Israel.

After 15 May the efforts invested in obtaining aircraft and arms elsewhere began to bear fruit. Al Schwimmer in the United States and Freddy Fredkins in Europe were making headway with their secret, mostly illegal purchases because of the arms embargo. Emissaries from Israel had also come to an arrangement with the Czechoslovakian government and, after getting a nod from the Soviet Union, bought Messerschmitt 109 fighter planes.

Three B-17 Flying Fortress heavy bombers, ten C-46 Curtiss Commando freighters, and three Lockeed Constellations were acquired in the United States. At night an airlift using C-54 Douglas Skymasters and C-46s from Czechoslovakia carried arms, and dismantled Messerschmitt fighters began arriving in Israel and saved the day. Slowly, the vitally necessary arms and aircraft began to augment the few aircraft that had arrived from South Africa.

MAHAL

Shortly after 15 May a stream of Mahal volunteers, mostly Jewish, arrived in appreciable numbers from South Africa, the United States, Canada, and Europe. The flow of volunteers was heartening, however, they encountered many problems. They had come from widely differing backgrounds and countries and arrived in the midst of a war for which they had not been prepared. Although in an unfamiliar environment with an unfamiliar language, they all were motivated by a desire to prevent the defeat and wholesale killing of the Jews of Palestine.

The Mahal volunteers were by and large from nontraditional Jewish homes. The stream of volunteers from different countries who left their homes and families to come to fight in the unfamiliar distant land was an expression of these Jews' longing for national identification with their people and its history.

Most had come without contracts, had not signed up for any fixed period, had nowhere to stay when they got leave, and were short of money. Having been the initiator of the first influx of foreign volunteers from South Africa and the commander of the first air force base, I tried to help them with their problems. I gathered more than a hundred volunteers in the Yarden Hotel lounge to discuss their problems.

In time steps were taken by the Zionist organizations in their home countries to supplement their meager army wages. The arrangements made by the South African Zionist Federation office in Tel Aviv became a role model for other countries. In the inevitable disorganization, which was a result of Israel's being thrust into a full-scale war before having the infrastructure of a state, there were even cases of overseas volunteers being killed in action without their families being informed or cared for.

It is of note that there was virtually no friction between the Mahalniks and the young local pilots, and relations between us and the small number of volunteers were excellent even in times of stress during the fighting.

MESSERSCHMITT OVER TEL AVIV

While the Egyptians enjoyed complete air superiority, we couldn't fly in daylight. Knowing that they did not fly their fighters at night, we began to take off just before sunset and land just after sunrise. We carried out many bombings of the southern Arab towns of Mijdal, Isdud, and Gaza, always at night but with limited results apart from the psychological effect on the Arabs and the lift to our morale. We faced anti-aircraft fire from light- and medium-caliber guns. After the Egyptians were entrenched in Gaza, the fire became more accurate with radar-controlled heavy guns and powerful searchlights.

One operation, which the population of Tel Aviv witnessed with a grandstand view, was a great morale builder. On 3 June 1948 two Egyptian Dakotas, converted to bombers, arrived over Tel Aviv. Despite the wailing of the air-raid sirens, we stood outside and watched in anger and frustration as without opposition they slowly circled and dropped their bombs. One bomb fell on the central bus station in Tel Aviv killing forty people and wounding more than a hundred. Undoubtedly, the Egyptians had been briefed by their intelligence that we had no fighters or anti-aircraft guns, and they were probably enjoying the easy raid. I was about to take off in desperation in a Bonanza with a man to operate a machine gun when we saw a fighter—one of our

Messerschmitts—approach the Dakotas from behind. Golden specks soon appeared around the big Daks.

Both Dakotas were hit by the Messerschmitt's fire and emitted streams of black smoke as they began losing height. The ME-109 continued to shoot at the two aircraft. The exhilaration of most of the raptly watching population of Tel Aviv was boundless. I took off immediately and followed the Dakota, which was attacked first, and saw it in a shallow dive flying south parallel to the coastline evidently still under pilot control. He made a crash-landing with wheels up on the beach near Bat Yam some ten kilometers south of Tel Aviv. I descended low over him flying into the cloud of oily, black smoke. Some of the crew survived and were taken prisoner.

This was the first shooting down of enemy aircraft by the Israel Air Force. The pilot of the Messerschmitt was Moddie Alon, who was destined to be my mate in 101 Squadron. It was the first interception by the Messerschmitt 109 fighters, which had just been airlifted from Czechoslovakia. After the downing of the two Daks, no more daylight bombing raids were carried out by enemy aircraft on any major population center in Israel. Some days before in the Bonanza, I had chased an enemy Anson bombing the outskirts of Ramat Gan with my driver in the back of the aircraft with his machine gun sticking out of the baggage door. We did not locate the light bomber. To be reduced to trying to down an attacking aircraft in a Bonanza with a machine gun firing through the open door of the rear baggage compartment best demonstrates our situation at that time.

AMMAN

At the beginning of June, orders came to bomb Amman, the capital of Transjordan. Ezra Omer, adjutant to General Dori, brought the operational order to me personally as commander of the base at Sde Dov. Ezra was a tall Sabra who was curt in his ways and not one to mince words; he had been through too many battles on the ground.

As we were still wary of flying during daylight hours in our defenseless aircraft, I planned the mission for night. I decided to fly the Bonanza myself, with another pilot flying one of the Fairchild light planes.

The Rapide pilot refused to fly the slow twin-engine biplane as he was afraid of being attacked by enemy fighters on the way back from the target, though we were fairly sure that no enemy fighter could intercept us at night. There was some justification in his refusal, especially as the slow Rapide would have been an easy target for an Egyptian Spitfire. Ezra Omer was present. He pulled out his pistol and, after putting it to the pilot's head, calmly said, "If you do not fly you get a bullet in your head." The pilot climbed into the Rapide without another word and took off to carry out the mission.

I took off first in the Bonanza carrying incendiaries to pinpoint the target, as the Pathfinders had done during the heavy bomber raids on German cities during World War II. The incendiaries were homemade, like all our bombs, but looked more professional—long sticks of shiny metal in hexagonal form. They were not heavy and could be tossed out of the aircraft with ease.

South African Dov Judah accompanied me to throw out the incendiaries. He had arrived as a Mahal volunteer early in the war and was prepared to carry out any duty, even as a lowly bomb-chucker during the early days of his service. He was a capable airman and later on in the war was appointed chief of operations of the air force. He was a Johannesburg lawyer and formerly a World War II SAAF navigator in B-26 Marauder bombers in Italy. He was about thirty, tough and uncompromising, and I had frequent contact with him through the war.

We headed southeast and crossed the Jordan River into Transjordan. Not a light was to be seen below, only the moonlight and glitter of stars keeping us company in the darkness beyond the glow of the instrument lights. The Dead Sea reflected the moonlight and the drone of the Lycoming engine was comforting as we flew deep into enemy territory in open formation.

We arrived over Amman after less than an hour. Surprisingly, there was no blackout, lights were blazing, and no anti-aircraft fire greeted us. We dropped our incendiary bombs, and almost immediately, all lights below were extinguished. Now anti-aircraft fire started. The flak was heavy but exploded below us. We circled while the others dropped their bombs near the fires lit by our incendiaries, and we headed home.

I was astonished to see in the distance that the strong beacon light of Lydda Airport in Transjordanian hands for some weeks was still in full operation a mere twenty kilometers from our home base at Sde Dov. It was the best navigational aid we could have wished for, and the irony of our bombing their capital and then returning to base with such splendid assistance caused some hilarity in the cockpit as we munched the chocolate bars I always carried on raids.

The raid caused little damage in Amman but generated panic. On our side news of the first raid on an Arab capital raised morale. Three of our bombs fell on the Royal Air Force base outside Amman damaging the main hangar that housed two of King Abdullah's Anson communications aircraft. One of the bombs did not explode, and the RAF sent it to the Air Ministry in London for examination and, if possible, an explanation for the large iron handle welded to its side. Had the Jews introduced a secret weapon to that theater of war? All our 50-kilo bombs were so equipped, but who outside the Israel Air Force had ever needed steel handles welded to bombs to help chuck them out?

Following the Amman raid the RAF gave orders to prepare for a fight with the Israel Air Force should another attack materialize. As no further incidents involving the RAF in Transjordan followed, nothing ever came of this order until the engagements in Sinai in January 1949 when the RAF clashed with the Israel Air Force and lost five fighter aircraft to Israel's 101 Squadron as described further on.

OVER CAIRO

When we heard that three B-17 four-engine bombers had been bought in the United States and flown to Czechoslovakia to be overhauled and equipped, I was ordered as deputy chief of operations to plan a bombing raid on Cairo. We had no good maps of Cairo and had to make do with tourist brochures. Study of these showed that the Defense Ministry, the Abdin Palace, and the Ministry of Foreign Affairs were in a straight line running from southwest to northeast of the city, and I chose them as targets. Israel lies well north of Egypt, therefore, I planned the approach to Cairo from the south as if coming from southern Egypt or Sudan. I felt the Egyptians would not suspect an unidentified aircraft approaching from the south. I prepared an operational order and took it to Czechoslovakia to brief the crews who were to bomb Cairo on their delivery flight to Israel.

I flew in a Lockheed Constellation of the Israel Air Force with a young American transport captain, Larry Raab. Our course to Czechoslovakia from Israel was via Corsica where we refueled. This refueling arrangement in Corsica and the tacit cooperation of the French at that time allowed the undercover airlift to exist. From there it was only about three hours to Czechoslovakia.

This was my first visit to Czechoslovakia and to the Israeli arms airlift base in the ancient village of Zatec. I was astonished to find in Zatec, behind the communist Iron Curtain, an airfield occupied by Israeli liaison men and a boisterous crowd of hard-drinking airmen, mostly American Jews. The leader of the American B-17 crews was a powerfully built former New York policeman, Ray Kurtz.

He was a bit older than me and very self-confident. When we met at the Stalingrad Hotel and I introduced myself he said, "No one is going to tell me where to fly my aircraft." He then ignored both me and the written operational order

I had brought. Such was discipline at that wild time, for there were no ranks and no real command structure in the air force. Orders were carried out by persuasion or threats. In this case the fact that I was a fighter pilot did not help much either for these were bomber pilots with their own opinions about fighter pilots. We had very little contact after the initial cold shoulder he gave me, but he eventually obeyed my operational orders regarding the approach to the target as well as the targets themselves.

The B-17s took off on the raid shortly after I arrived back in Israel. They flew in loose formation from Zatec to the Adriatic, on the way edging into Albanian airspace. The Albanian anti-aircraft batteries fired at them to no effect, then they headed out to sea. There was oxygen in only one of the bombers, and it made for the main target of Cairo at high altitude while the other two bombed the Egyptian air base at El Arish. There were other mishaps on the flight including one near-fatal event. A crew member, trying to repair a fault in the bomb bay of one of the B-17s, fell and got stuck in one of the bomb bays with half of his body hanging out below the fuselage at 12,000 feet. He held on for dear life while the slipstream buffeted and tugged at his body, but the crew managed to pull him back into the aircraft.

FAROUK OFF THE TEL AVIV COAST

Chief of Staff Yigael Yadin's younger brother was Mattie Sukenik. He was a tall, sandy-haired young Sabra with a light brown mustache. He was one of the early Palmach pilots and I had taken an immediate liking to him. Unfortunately, he was washed out of his Palmach pilot's course when it was discovered that he was color blind, and I took him as my bomb-chucker. He sat beside me on raids holding the bombs on his lap and twirling his long mustache as he waited for my signal to throw the bombs over the side. He had to arm the bombs by pulling a fuse, sometimes with an alarming audible detonation when we arrived over the target. He would then throw the bombs out of the right-hand window or through the luggage-loading hatch behind me. In those days I had contact on a daily basis with his brother Yigael Yadin who once confided to me that he was sure nothing would happen to his brother as long as he flew with me. Those were prophetic words.

We normally went on bombing missions with either the window or the right-hand door removed. In the earlier missions, we did the chucking ourselves, but later on found it better to employ someone especially for that purpose. When we approached Kfar Etzion while it was surrounded and cut off from the rest of the Yishuv, we had to dive low to deliver ammunition and medical supplies. Our missions often had mixed results owing to inaccurate dropping. Later on, bomb racks with electrical releases were fitted on the Bonanza; they provided much greater accuracy. I began to fly without a bomb-chucker.

Early in June 1948, Mattie and I were lunching at Café Kassit on Dizengoff Street. By this time the two bomb racks fitted under the fuselage of my Bonanza made possible much more accurate bombing and Mattie was flying as bomb-chucker with other pilots. Suddenly a waiter came up to me saying, "There is an urgent message for you from general headquarters." I hurried to the phone and was shocked to hear that Egyptian vessels were heading for the Tel Aviv coast in an attempt to land invading troops. The threat meant that we were in serious danger, for apart from the token forces of the Kiryati Brigade, there were no troops available to meet an invasion in the Tel Aviv area. Obviously, the Egyptians possessed enough intelligence information to know that this populous heart of the Jewish state couldn't defend itself against a combined operation landing.

I ran to my Jeep. Mattie had just learned to drive, and he begged me to let him drive me to the airfield. I did not refuse him, though I knew that he had been driving only a short time. Sadly that decided his fate.

I telephoned general headquarters, and we agreed that I would carry out a reconnaissance to give them a report of what was happening. I took off in the Bonanza, and as I crossed the coast I saw below me a small ship of ours wallowing slowly toward the west with one man on the bridge manning a solitary machine gun. The air force was not the only branch of the Israeli forces that had to make do with ridiculously inadequate weapons.

We climbed to 2,000 feet, and I was shaken to see less than six kilometers from the coast a naval flotilla approaching Tel Aviv. The invading force consisted of one large naval vessel, a tank-landing craft, and an escort ship. As soon as my aircraft approached, they turned to face me and I saw from their wake that they had increased their speed. The large ship, which I subsequently discovered was the flagship of the Egyptian navy, was well equipped with anti-aircraft guns. As soon as I approached, the sky was filled with shell bursts. I circled out of range of their guns and had a good look at them. It was amusing to see the three large vessels increasing to maximum speed and turning to face my relatively harmless Bonanza every time I headed to them from a different angle. I decided to attack them and, after climbing to 4,000 feet, went into a steep turn and dived. Throughout the encounter we were so close to shore that the Tel Aviv beachfront was in full view.

I released my two bombs and pulled up and away from the exploding anti-aircraft shells in a weaving skidding pattern. When I had settled down out of range of their guns, I circled and observed the results, noting the explosions of my two bombs in the water close to the flagship but probably not near enough to do any damage. I returned to Sde Dov, reported my findings to general headquarters, and bombed up for another sortie. There were a mere thirty minutes between sorties. The second attempt was better, for one bomb landed in the water close to the big flagship and the second was a direct hit on the ship. The vessel slowed appreciably and ceased turning to face me as I flew around it, indicating that the steering was damaged.

On returning to the field, I sent off our twin-engine Rapide carrying a large number of small bombs, which it dropped in a long stick. In the Fairchild I sent one of the young ex-Palmach pilots, David Sprinzak, accompanied by Mattie as bomb-chucker. After two approaches the Fairchild suddenly plunged into the sea. I went out to search for it but found only wreckage floating on the sea near the shore. My bomb-chucker partner Mattie died when he should have been off duty but, instead, insisted on driving me to the airfield.

Recently, I learned that Mattie and David were probably shot down by a Hawker Fury fighter-bomber on loan from the Iraqi Air Force after radio calls for assistance from the flagship to their El Arish air force base. In Independence Park in Tel Aviv, there is a large statue dedicated to the fly-ers of 1948. It was put up some fifteen years after Mattie and David were shot down. It is close to the shore near the water where they were hit, and for me it is a memorial to David and Mattie. I pass by it occasionally and it still haunts me. To this day I have a clear image in my mind of dear Mattie sitting beside me during our drops of ammunition and medical supplies to Kfar Etzion. I picture him waving and blowing kisses to the kibbutzniks from the opening on his side of the aircraft.

Because my Bonanza was the only one fitted with an elec-trical bomb rack, I know my bomb was the only one that hit the ship. After my bombing run, it turned sluggishly into a southerly direction and made slow progress at much re-duced speed toward the Ashkelon coast, where it was sunk by the brave men of the secret Flotilla Number 13 of the Israel Navy.

The morning after the battle with the Egyptian invasion force, I was having lunch at the Galey Yam restaurant on the sea front. It had a full view of the action that had taken place. Not all our volunteers from overseas were modest, committed young men. We had a few of the usual bull-shit-ters and boasters too. At the next table was a Mahal volunteer who was loudly relating how he had seen the whole action from the seafront the day before saying, "I would have attacked the Egyptian ships differently. I would have flown in at low level and skidded my bombs into the ships and not have tried to dive-bomb them. These guys don't know a thing about bombing a ship." I listened without saying a word. The efficacy of our attack was to be seen clearly with the limping flag ship wallowing away to the south and the others turning tail and escaping from the scene of the engagement as quickly as they could. I doubt whether the loud-mouthed volunteer had ever seen any action anywhere, and I did not subsequently see him flying from any of our airfields.

His boastful comments were not typical of the volunteers who came to help during Israel's baptism of fire. Most of them were fighters deeply committed to the survival of the Israeli homeland 2,000 years after Rome completed the conquest of Judea.

No doubt, some of the volunteers were seeking adventure and escape from their humdrum civilian lives after they had been fighting in World War II, but the majority were fired by idealistic motives. One would have expected that, among the pilots who had not long before been on active service in the allied forces, there might been much flotsam and jetsam from the war years. It is surprising that, on the contrary, the human material that came was made up largely of dedicated volunteers.

In general, expectations were to a large extent colored by what had been told by those who recruited them. There was a minimum of friction and disappointment among the volunteers from South Africa. I was in the fortunate position of having been in the Air Service before returning to South Africa to recruit the first batch of volunteers. I had been careful to impress upon everyone that there would be virtually no pay and that conditions would be Spartan in the extreme.

The recruits from South Africa were the first Mahal volunteers to arrive and were the forerunners of many hundreds who came in the following months to take part in the War of Independence. It is also of note that, by chance, the three aircraft that foiled the attempted Egyptian invasion of the Tel Aviv shore were among those purchased in far-off South Africa. They had survived the difficult flight up the African continent to Israel and the Egyptian bombings of Sde Dov on 15 May.

On 11 June 1948, shortly after the attempted invasion of Tel Aviv, a truce was declared between Israel and the Arabs. Two days later, a large white DC-3 was seen approaching Sde Dov from the southeast. Our anti-aircraft gunners took up positions for we were on edge expecting more attacks from the Egyptians. I barely had time to get them to hold fire when a transport with the letters KLM printed largely on its fuselage landed. When the door of the aircraft opened, two passengers made their way down the steps.

Not knowing who they were, I greeted the man who was evidently the leader as graciously as possible under the circumstances. He was a tall, slim man with cold, blue eyes, and he looked somewhat disdainfully at my armband. No one in the Israel forces yet had ranks or insignia, and I had ordered a dark blue armband with red Hebrew lettering stating "field commander" and another for my squadron commander. The leader's companion was dark skinned and for some reason I decided (erroneously) that he was one of ours, perhaps someone from the Foreign Office.

Still mystified, I served them tea in my office. After a while a message came that the tall man was Count Folke Bernadotte, the Swedish United Nations mediator. Being so far removed both in time and geography from my skiing trip to Sweden in 1945, and in the stiff, formal atmosphere that prevailed during this meeting, I did not mention that I had met his niece and we had become friendly while we were on that skiing holiday.

I summoned the largest taxi I had at the field and told the driver to take them to the Gat Rimon, which was the best hotel in Tel Aviv at the time. As I accompanied them to the vehicle, I dropped behind so that I could have a word with the dark-skinned gentleman. I complained about not having received any indication from headquarters as to what to do with Count Bernadotte. I didn't realize he was the second UN mediator, Dr. Ralph Bunche.

Bernadotte was assassinated shortly afterward near Jerusalem, by the Stern Group, the most radical of the underground forces. Later it was explained to me that they had managed to gain access to one of his diaries and that the Stern Group suspected him of being an anti-Semite, who was planning to sell us down the river to the Arabs. I doubt if there is any agreement about his true role, though in the short time I spent with him he was cold and unfriendly.

ALTALENA

My final encounter with the Irgun occurred in June 1948. It was right after the Irgun had reached agreement about joining the newly established Israeli armed forces. In the preceding months, the Irgun had been busy with massive acquisitions of arms in Europe for its units in Israel. The main object of the arms acquisition was for use in the battle for the Old City of Jerusalem. The Irgun made a deal with the French government according to which the Irgun would be allowed to load men, arms, and armed cars on a 5,000-ton vessel, the *Altalena*, at port in France. The vessel had been used in World War II as a tank landing craft. The Irgun promised support for France in its conflict in the Maghreb. The French were unhappy at having been ousted from their traditional role in Syria and Lebanon, and were not adverse to helping anti-British forces. Everything was done in absolute secrecy. Discovery of the *Altalena* project by the Arabs would have been a serious blow because it was breaking the Anglo-American embargo on the passage of arms and military personnel to the Middle East.

On the night of 19 June, the *Altalena* arrived off the Israel coast and made for Kfar Vitkin, a settlement forty kilometers north of Tel Aviv. The Israeli Prime Minister Ben Gurion knew of the ship's pending arrival, but differences between the Irgun and Ben Gurion arose concerning the agreement between the Irgun and the government about distribution of the arms. Because of misunderstandings, which had their roots in the deep antagonism that had ex-

isted for years between the Haganah and the Irgun, a pro-
foundly sad situation developed. The Irgun wanted to use
the arms and the personnel for their comrades who were
fighting desperately against the Arabs in Jerusalem. They refused to hand over control of the ship and its contents to
the legitimate government. Based on mutual distrust, Ben
Gurion and the army chiefs feared a coup d'état by the
Irgun. A force of 600 soldiers was sent to Kfar Vitkin and
the army refused to let the *Altalena* unload its cargo of arms
and volunteers. Shots were fired at the Irgun fighters and
the Israel Navy vessels fired at the *Altalena*. The volunteers
on board the Altalena returned fire.

While all this was going on, I was asleep in the Yarden
Hotel in Tel Aviv, exhausted as usual from the endless night
flying. I was awakened by someone who told me what was
going on and warned me there were rumors the Irgun was
about to try to take over control of Israel. The news was so
incredible that I believed it only when I saw an armed soldier posted outside my door to protect me, as commander
of the main air unit of the country, from the Irgun.

This bizarre situation in which I, as a secret member of
the Irgun, was being guarded and protected from the Irgun
by the army was untenable. Feverishly, I sought a way out
of the dilemma. I got into my staff car and rushed to the
headquarters of the Irgun in the former Freund Hospital on
Lilienblum Street in Tel Aviv. As I drove alone through the
darkened streets of the city, I tried desperately to find a so-
lution. Only an occasional military police vehicle could be
seen.

I found the Irgun headquarters in darkness; there were

no guards at the entrance. It seemed deserted, but I found one of Begin's deputies, Haim Landau, seated alone at an old-fashioned switchboard. I said, "Haim Landau, I am being guarded against a supposed coup d'état by the Irgun. What is going on?" He looked at me in astonishment and said, "I don't know anything. It's ridiculous. All I know is that there has been some shooting at Kfar Vitkin, and Begin has gone there to clarify matters."

I returned to my quarters at the Yarden Hotel, where the night porter told me there was an urgent call for me to telephone general headquarters. I drove to Sde Dov, and from the operations room got on to headquarters. I was ordered to prepare three aircraft immediately to bomb the *Altalena*. Now my predicament was overwhelming. On the one hand, I had to obey orders from my commanders, but no force on earth could have made me bomb the Irgun ship with its complement of Jewish volunteers. Later, I discovered that the former leader of the Irgun forces in Europe, my close friend "Benjamin," was in command of the *Altalena*.

I set about locating two other pilots, who unknown to anyone in the air force, were former Irgun members. Ezer was not available. Fortune smiled, for two of them were nearby in Tel Aviv and I brought them to Sde Dov quickly. I was not sure what I would do when the order came to bomb the ship. I considered various stratagems such as deliberately missing the target or sabotaging the aircraft before takeoff.

I consented grudgingly when, an hour later, an order came to fly over the ship and circle it while flashing navigation lights without dropping bombs. I took off and made my way along the coastline in the pitch-black darkness, the sea and the sky merging in the pervading gloom. I thought of my comrades far below in the blackness, surrounded and embattled by their own government's troops. Now they were about to be entombed in their ship at the very moment of their triumph, having finally reached Israel with their desperately needed arms and fighting personnel. I was in agony. No! I could never bomb my fellow Jews.

I circled the doomed ship in an airplane belonging to forces on the point of ordering me to bomb the ship and its Irgun volunteers, some of whom only some months before had been my blood brothers and comrades. Most fortunately, GHQ held back the order to bomb at the last minute. I returned to base and awaited another fateful order to bomb the ship. After some hours of tension, GHQ told me that it had finally decided not to bomb the ship. Believing a demonstration of strength by flying over the ship while flashing my navigation lights would be an effective warning to the men below, I was ordered to do so.

During the confusion at Kfar Vitkin, Begin boarded the ship and remained on it until the end. The *Altalena* did not complete the unloading at Kfar Vitkin and was deliberately beached on the shore of Tel Aviv in full view of the city's population, the UN observers, and the world media. The *Altalena* was fired upon and destroyed after a direct order from Ben Gurion. For months the rusting, blackened hulk on the lovely beachfront of Tel Aviv bore mute testimony to man's folly.

I was relieved when an order came for me to proceed to Czechoslovakia for a conversion course on the Messerschmitt 109. The order came while the *Altalena* was sailing from Kfar Vitkin to the Tel Aviv beach, and I was spared the necessity of being an unhappy star player in the confrontation between the government forces and the Irgun. I heard later that when the Mahal aircrews were told to load aircraft for a possible action against the *Altalena* there was a revolt against being involved in any action against Jews.

The *Altalena* became the target of artillery, and Jews killed Jews on the burning ship or as they jumped into the sea. Sorely needed military equipment was destroyed in the fire, which gutted the ship. The pall of smoke from the *Altalena* was like a funeral pyre in front of where the Dan Hotel now stands in Tel Aviv. It put an end to the saddest chapter in Israel's rebirth. During the confrontation nineteen people were killed, sixteen of them Irgun fighters.

The *Altalena* affair left a deep and lasting schism between the two opposing factions in Israel. Being a secret member of the Irgun but serving in the air arm of the Haganah, I was in a better position than most at the time to make an impartial judgment. My opinion is that both the Irgun and Prime Minister Ben Gurion were unreasonably paranoid about the whole question leading to the dispute. Both Ben Gurion and Begin played their hands badly. Begin's refusal to bow to government authority in Israel was unacceptable and had to be opposed. However, I feel that Ben Gurion's misreading of Begin's intentions was the main cause of the tragedy that followed in plain view of Israel's population and the world media.

My last meeting with Begin was years later in Jerusalem at a party to launch his book *White Night*. By this time I was an active supporter of the Peace Now Movement, which encouraged a policy of compromise with the Arabs in order to arrive at a peace settlement. During the reception someone told Begin. This news must have been both surprising and distasteful for him, but he took it with equanimity. He came up to me and said, "We are all free people who have their own choice." He accompanied his statement with a big hug.

Not long thereafter in May 1977, Begin won the elections and became prime minister of Israel, bringing into his government Ezer as minister of defense, Dayan as foreign minister, and Yadin as deputy prime minister, all having been generals during Ben Gurion's reign. For me this closed the gap in my strange allegiance to the two opposing forces.

THE MULE

Following the purchase of twenty-five new Czech-built World War II German fighters, our pilots were sent to Czechoslovakia for training. After seven had completed the first course, I went with the second batch. When we arrived at the Czechoslovak base of Ceske Budejovice, I was encouraged to find my comrades. In the course were South African and American volunteers, a great follow-on to the few men recruited in Johannesburg earlier. Here, too, I met the American volunteer George Lichter, who has been my lifelong friend and fighter-pilot comrade both in Israel and since he returned to his home in New York.

By the time we arrived in Prague, the communists had

infiltrated every facet of the economy. We quickly learned that the Czech expression for the nationalized businesses was "Narodni Podnik." The best nightclub in Prague where one could get fine steaks and desserts with whipped cream was "Monica," and it also belonged to the communist administration The hotels had all the appurtenances of a Western capitalist establishment, which jarred with one's image of communism. However, that was no concern of ours and, as long as the Czechs were willing to lend support to our budding air force, we accepted the anomalies in their system happily.

I took with me twenty U.S. dollars, which I changed on the free market at 400 crowns per dollar. The official rate was fifty. The small sum I had brought in dollars, once converted at the free market rate, supplied me with all my requirements—two recorded symphonies, a set of Bohemian glassware, and a number of books about Russia, which were freely and cheaply available in the shops compliments of the Soviet propaganda machine.

České Budějovice was a Czech Air Force training base in eastern Czechoslovakia, and we were outfitted with flying overalls, helmets, and gloves. The irony of the situation was not lost on me, for here we were, Jewish pilots in the Israel Air Force, training on German Messerschmitt 109s, wearing Nazi Luftwaffe flying suits. To top it all, we were flying behind the Iron Curtain. A greater irony was that several of us had flown Spitfires in combat against Nazi Messerschmitts in World War II and were now about to fly Messerschmitts in missions against Spitfires of the Egyptian Air Force.

Our accommodations at the air base were basic but adequate. Tins of food from the Israeli embassy in Prague supplemented the meager Czech military rations. The camp food consisted mainly of suet dumplings with a meat sauce and was not the kind of fare we were used to after an Israeli diet lavishly supplemented with fresh vegetables and salads.

In addition to the food in the mess, we were given Czech ration coupons. Though we did not encounter the shortages endemic in an economy based on central government control, the dissatisfaction of most of the population with the regime after the communist putsch was evident on all sides and was probably the main reason for the warmth we encountered from the Czech people. Mainly because of the language barriers, we had little contact with the Czechs apart from our flying instructors. The chief instructor at České Budějovice was Captain Bilek, a man of somewhat surly demeanor. The instructors were always correct and businesslike in their attitude to us and would never discuss politics.

We began our training in the German Arado trainer to become familiar with the airfield, followed by a short spell in a two-seater Messerschmitt with Captain Bilek. Having served in the Czech branch of the Royal Air Force in England during World War II, he spoke English fairly well. We avoided straying into Austrian air space as the border was close to the base. That would have been a catastrophe, for the Americans occupying Austria at that time would have learned of our presence and what we were doing in České Budějovice. In the political climate of the Cold War, it might well have put an end to the whole Czechoslovakian program.

My first flight in the Czech-built Messerschmitt 109 was not encouraging. It was rightly called the Mule, for taking off and landing in one piece was an achievement. It had an unpleasant built-in swing during these phases, and ten of the twenty-six that were brought to Israel were written off either on landing or takeoff, despite being piloted by experienced World War II fighter pilots. I was among the few who did not damage a Messerschmitt. The reason for the swing was the narrow undercarriage and the heavy torque from the Junkers Jumo engine with its outsized paddle-bladed propeller. The original German-built Messerschmitts handled better with the more-powerful Daimler Benz engine and a normal prop.

The Messerschmitt was a poor substitute for the Spitfire, which some of us knew firsthand, but all knew it was a formidable fighting machine with its two 20mm cannon and two 12.7mm machine guns, and was our first real fighter. The Egyptians were terrified of it, probably attributing our constant victories to the aircraft, whereas, in fact, our success came from our World War II experience.

The absence of any armor protection behind the pilot's seat, common in all fighter planes from the West, created an impression of lack of care for the pilot. The seat was low in a semi-reclining position, and it was alarming when the leading-edge flaps sprung out in steep turns. Another unnerving feature of the Czech fighters was that, although there were two 20mm cannon in the wings, there were two machine guns, which fired through the propeller. In theory, that was fine, but when the synchronization failed, as happened more than once in the squadron, you shot off your own propeller. Apart from these unpleasant characteristics, the aircraft had a fair performance, and during dogfights with Egyptian Spitfires, we always came out on top. Despite the Mule's problems, I was happy to be facing the enemy at last in a real fighter aircraft.

After the course we flew back to Israel in one of the airlift cargo planes via Ajaccio in Corsica again, with pleasant memories of Czechoslovakia and the warmth of its people's attitude toward us at that critical time when no other country was willing to extend us a hand of friendship. I am not the only one with fond memories of that small, formerly communist country in central Europe. It should be remembered by the Jews of the world that both Russian permission for the Czechs to assist us as well as Russian diplomatic and political support in the United Nations during that period were instrumental in helping Israel to survive.

ISRAELI SPITFIRE

Before coming to agreement with the Czech government to purchase Messerschmitts, we explored every possibility of acquiring fighter planes that could oppose the Egyptian Air Force. We tried buying fighters from all over the world without success. But when the British forces left Palestine after the end of the Mandate, they left scrap heaps of discarded and damaged aircraft. Some of our technical personnel were familiar with the Spitfire from their RAF service during World War II. After the fighting began and the first Egyptian Spitfires were shot down, work was begun in earnest on building a Spitfire from scrap. A set of wings and a fuselage belonging to different marks of Spitfire were found. The wings were from a photo-reconnaissance Spit, and the fuselage from a Mark IX. The leading spirits behind the rebuilding of the Spitfire were two ex-RAF mechanics I knew. When the aircraft was finally ready for a test flight, no pilot in 101 Squadron had sufficient confidence in the mechanics who built it to test-fly it. Though I was in headquarters at the time, I jumped at the chance to test-fly our first Spitfire and offered to make the test flight. The pilots of 101 Squadron stood near the runway at Herzlia as I prepared to take off.

I did not mention to anyone that I had never flown a Spitfire IX, having only done a conversion course on Spitfire VBs in 1944 in Egypt. I had not flown a World War II fighter for nearly three years. When I climbed into the cockpit and strapped myself in, I did have twinges of anxiety, but the mechanics had done an outstanding job in rebuilding without manuals or technical literature about Spitfires.

The takeoff was typical of the Spitfire, as I remembered it from my time in Egypt. I was off the ground swiftly, and it was great to fly a Spitfire again. She behaved perfectly and I flew her to Kibbutz Ma'abarot near Natanya. The field was not operational and was unknown even to most of the air force pilots. We had decided to keep secret the existence of an Israeli Spitfire and hid her there among trees. The rousing cheers of the ground staff lining the sides of the runway when I landed made me feel good, and I was happy to fly the first Spitfire with Israel Air Force markings.

I subsequently heard that there was a state of dejection among the fighter pilots in 101 Squadron for they had seen me take off in the Spit after a short run of barely 300 meters, whereas the Messerschmitts needed most of the 800-meter runway to get airborne.

This lone Spit—number 10 was the number given to it by the Israel Air Force—was to be a secret weapon for a while. It enabled me to carry out photo-reconnaissance missions deep behind the Egyptian lines with confidence, for the enemy did not know our secret and, therefore, were unlikely to attack a lone Spit far behind their lines. It provided a safe camera platform for us for many months.

The first mission for the Spit was escort to a light photo-reconnaissance aircraft. A plan had been hatched at general headquarters to introduce an armored division through the extreme south of the country from the Red Sea. For this purpose, it was essential to photograph the present situation of all the oases in the Arava Valley, which stretched from what is now Eilat up to the Dead Sea. As mentioned earlier I had done the one long flight down as far as the Red Sea some months before, but as matters began to heat up and our procurement possibilities improved, the question of a landing from the extreme south became more feasible. We decided to reconnoiter all the oases in the deep south.

At this time, volunteer aircrews were arriving on every Universal Airlines flight from Johannesburg. One of these was Monty Goldberg, a member of a family with whom I had been friendly since my early youth. He had been an experienced aerial photographer in the South African Air Force. When I got the order to organize the reconnaissance and photographing of all the oases between Sdom on the Dead Sea and Aqaba on the Red Sea, I chose Monty. The only aircraft suitable for the purpose was the high-wing Fairchild, ideal for photography but a sitting duck for any fighter.

I chose a pilot named Paltiel Makleff to fly Monty down into the Negev desert. As the Fairchild was unarmed and flying into enemy territory, I planned to escort them in the Spitfire. I flew the Spit to the base at Tel Nof to join Monty and Paltiel. Before takeoff, Paltiel complained of a magneto drop in the Fairchild engine. By that time I had had a number of cases of pilots complaining of mag drops before takeoff on a mission, usually by pilots with nerves at breaking point. I replied, "Mag drop or no mag drop, you take off."

Because of the impossibility of giving close escort with the Spitfire's much higher flying speed, I waited at the beginning of the runway for about twenty minutes after the Fairchild's takeoff, the time I needed to meet it and circle above when it entered enemy territory.

My engine overheated, not an uncommon occurrence in Spitfires in the hot climate of the Middle East, and I was late in departing. By the time I reached our rendevous point, Monty and Paltiel were nowhere to be seen, and I was forced to return to base when my fuel ran low. Eventually, a message arrived reporting they had completed part of their mission, but about sixty kilometers from the base at Tel Nof, they had force-landed in Arab territory with engine trouble and were now prisoners of war.

So the magneto drop was real. Here was another case of my sending a close friend out on a mission from which he did not return. In this case they both survived. I met Monty many years later in Johannesburg, and though I was a little apprehensive, he was overjoyed to see me again and bore no grudge. Monty and Paltiel were fortunate to have survived, for when they landed, it was in territory under the control of Arab irregulars, who took off their shoes and whipped them into a mad run. Fortunately, an Egyptian army officer appeared, took charge, and moved them to a prisoner-of-war camp in Egypt, where they were treated reasonably. They were in the prison camp until the end of the war in early 1949 and then returned to Israel.

In the last days of December 1948, when our Seventh Brigade crossed the Egyptian-Israeli border in the far south on its way to the main Egyptian forward air base at El Arish, they found another Spitfire in one of the revetments at the nearby El Arish satellite airfield. I had bombed the field a few times and noted that there were aircraft in revetments and parked around the field under camouflage netting.

I drove in a jeep to the satellite field, on the way passing near Kurnub, the only location in that very dry part of the world that sported a large and deep pool of water. It is now the site of the town of Dimona. At the satellite field, I was surprised to see what appeared to be eight Spitfires under camouflage netting. With only one exception, however, they were dummies. We had been deceived into bombing the field when it contained mainly dummy aircraft.

I climbed into the only real Spitfire, switched on the ignition, and was surprised to see the ignition light shining. I tried a number of times to get it started, but couldn't. I had to leave it with the ground troops evacuating the area hurriedly because of returning Egyptian forces. In fact, while I was trying to start the Spitfire, I heard shelling nearby, proving the situation was still fluid. There was little that could be done, but I refused to leave the precious Spit there. The army had a spare command car available, and we hooked the tail wheel of the airplane over the back of the vehicle and began to tow it to our lines. After an hour or two of towing, there was nothing more I could do to help and I hitched a ride back to Tel Aviv. Near Beersheba, a vehicle coming the other way knocked off the wing. Fortunately, it was not a total loss, for it was repaired and entered service eventually with 101 Squadron.

After capturing the main airfield of El Arish, we found the Egyptians had already evacuated most of their aircraft before our ground troops reached it and had torched all the unserviceable aircraft that could not be evacuated. In the canal zone, RAF bases refueled Egyptian Air Force planes, which were landing at their fields on their way back to Egypt during the period when they were in full retreat. So much for British neutrality during our war of survival with the Arab states in 1948.

VELVETA

British Spitfire fighters were inherited by the Czech squadrons that served with the RAF in World War II and were taken to Czechoslovakia after the war. After the communist takeover in 1948, the Czechs had to alter the anomalous situation of having an air force equipped with British fighters. Israel was still desperately short of fighter aircraft, having less than a dozen Messerschmitts left of the original twenty-six. We decided to buy forty Spitfires, which the Czechs undertook to prepare for the long flight to Israel.

I went to Czechoslovakia to initiate the ferrying to Israel of the Spitfires. The ferry operation was code-named "Velveta," and the Israel Navy was brought into the planning. Rescue vessels were stationed in the Mediterranean to patrol the route the aircraft would use, flying from Kunevice near Uherske Radice in the eastern half of Czechoslovakia. There were no runways, and the landing area was a large grass field. This airfield's overhaul facilities carried out repairs and final adjustments to the Spitfires after stripping them of all armament and anything not essential for flight.

As the Spitfire's normal maximum range was 700 kilometers, and Israel is 2,500 kilometers from Czechoslovakia, a major problem arose. Sam Pomerantz, a former engineer in the U.S. Army Air Forces, and a dedicated Mahal volunteer, undertook to equip them with long-range fuel tanks under the wings. The only fuel tanks available were drop tanks from Messerschmitts, so Sam headed a team in Prague, which set to work modifying the Spits to take the Messerschmitt's tanks. He designed and equipped the tanks with a feed system to enable the pilot to pump fuel from the extra tanks into the standard tank under the belly of the aircraft. He then installed small pumps for operation by the pilot during the flight. Gauges screwed into the right wall of the cockpit indicated the fuel quantity left in the slipper tank underneath the aircraft. As the level dropped, the pilot operated the pump, transferring the fuel. The British designers of the legendary Spitfire with its glorious history in World War II would have turned over in their graves if they had seen us in their beloved Spits cruising blithely over the Mediterranean with a Messerschmitt tank under each wing. Even with this extended range, however, we couldn't reach Israel nonstop from Kunevice, so an intermediate refueling stop was essential.

As there was no other country along the direct route that would permit us to fly over it, let alone to refuel, we negotiated an agreement with Yugoslavia to refuel in their country. At that time Marshal Tito had severed ties with the Soviets, and as there was as yet no contact with the Western powers, the Yugoslav Air Force couldn't get aviation-grade fuel from either the Russians or the West. Israel undertook to provide the Yugoslavs with aviation fuel, and in return, they granted the Israel Air Force a refueling base on the long flight to Israel.

A base codenamed "Yoram" was set up on a dried lake at Nikšić near Titograd in Montenegro. We were briefed that, in case of a forced-landing, we were to contact the UDBA (Yugoslav Gestapo) and ask for Gedda (an Israeli pilot formerly in the RAF). Gedda Shochat, a powerfully built, hearty member of Kibbutz Kfar Gileadi in northern Israel, was the man responsible for our contacts with the Yugoslavs. He was the one who saw to the equipping of the airfield for us. After arrival, the Spits were to refuel and continue over the Greek Peloponnese to the Mediterranean and on to Israel.

As such a long-range flight had never been attempted before in a Spitfire, an Israel Air Force four-engine DC-4 Skymaster crew would navigate and lead the fighters. An experienced South African volunteer navigator was chosen for the Skymaster. He was to calculate the fuel remaining in each Spitfire, instruct the pilots by radio as to their exact position, and tell them if they were going to make it or should turn back.

Six of us were to fly this first batch of Spitfires. Overhaul of the aircraft and checking the Messerschmitt-tank additions took weeks. One evening, after returning from dinner in one of the few restaurants in the area, we found the female manager of our hotel standing at the front entrance awaiting us and sobbing. Two men were standing next to her wearing long, black leather overcoats. They were from the secret police.

They wanted to know who we were and what we were doing there. They insisted on coming upstairs with us to examine our rooms and belongings. They gestured to us to open our suitcases and poked among our belongings. We were incensed and demanded identification. They seemed to be surprised at our demand, obviously not having been questioned in the past. They turned up the collars of their black leather coats to reveal Czech secret police badges. Matters looked dire for us when they found our revolvers, issued by the Israeli embassy in Prague.

Obviously, they had not been informed we were persona grata as far as their government was concerned. The end of the incident came quickly when, at our insistence, they telephoned their bosses, who told them what we were doing in Kunevice. The panic and tears of our host gave us an idea of what life was like under a communist regime.

One of our six pilots was Tuksie Blau, a young South African I had recruited with the first batch of volunteers. He had little experience on advanced fighters, so I arranged for him to undergo a conversion course on Spitfires at Kunevice, and he managed it well. After the work on the Spitfires ended, we took off one early morning on a cloudless day in August departing in the six aircraft in fine style. We flew in loose formation from Czechoslovakia over Hungary to the Adriatic coast. I found it odd to be flying behind the Iron Curtain over one communist country after the other in Israel Air Force Spitfires.

The weather had been fair when we took off, but shortly after passing over Hungary, we ran into clouds. None of us had instrument ratings, there were no navigational aids, and after some time we had to break formation, with each pilot making for the field on his own. We reached Yoram in three hours and found the unmarked field in spite of the bad weather. I was the first to land, and I taxied my Spit toward a group of tents near a river on the west side of the stony dry field. Tuksie was following me, but forgot to lower his undercarriage and landed on the Spitfire's belly. He was uninjured but the Spit was a write-off. That meant one down and five to go.

I was particularly upset by the crash, for the Operations Department in Tel Aviv had sent Arnie Ruch, an experienced South African Spitfire pilot to fly the sixth Spit. I had insisted that Tuksie fly it for he had passed the conversion course on to Spitfires successfully. Moreover, he had been waiting around for weeks, bored stiff by the inactivity. I had no doubt that he would manage the flight to Israel in company with the rest of us, but I am still bothered about my poor judgment.

The airfield at Yoram was in an exposed location surrounded by mountains and bounded on one side by a fast-flowing river. Apart from tents and a shack with a radio transceiver, there was nothing. We slept in tents on the desolate airfield, washed in the icy river nearby, and our food was mostly in tins from Israel. We were constantly under the watchful eyes of Yugoslavian soldiers, who did not allow any of us to leave the field. Every day, the soldiers sat on the ground in a circle under a Yugoslavian flag listening to an officer, who stood in the middle with a book in his hand. As we had no contact with these soldiers, it was anyone's guess as to whether these lectures were for general education or communist dogma.

After spending a week sitting around in the tents without a radio or news of the war in Israel, the C-54 appeared, made a few circuits to check the field, and then made a bumpy landing. Shortly after the landing, we received a radio message from Israel forecasting good weather en route. Soon we took off in the five Spitfires led by the Skymaster. We climbed to 8,000 feet in loose formation, three aircraft on one side of the Skymaster and two on the other. We flew in fine weather past Albania, over the Greek Peloponnese, to the Mediterranean. Soon the Greek islands appeared in the blue sea with the mountains of Turkey to port.

The beauty of the Mediterranean and the Greek islands

belied the tension we felt in our cramped cockpits while keeping the fuel gauges under constant scrutiny. Navigation was the responsibility of the Skymaster's navigator, who worked in the ideal conditions of a large aircraft with his navigation computer and radio link with Israel. We left it to him to worry about how much fuel we had left and whether it was enough for us to reach Israel.

Communication with the Skymaster was by VHF radio. The navigator in the lead aircraft constantly monitored our fuel consumption, getting radio reports from each of us as our slipper tanks ran dry. When the slipper tank ran completely dry and caused the engine to cut, we were to tell him so he could calculate our fuel consumption and decide whether our fuel reserve was sufficient for the remainder of the flight.

Using the last drop of fuel in our slipper tank before switching over to the main tanks in the wings meant a short period of fuel starvation. This method was a bit risky for there was a possibility that we would be unable to restart the engine after it cut, but we had no choice. Still acutely aware of what had happened to me in Venice, I made sure of my buoyancy in case I had to ditch or bale out over the sea by wearing two Mae West life jackets.

Between the islands of Rhodes and Cyprus, I saw the Spitfire of my mate Moddie Alon, who was on the left of the Skymaster, turn sharply and lose height. A few seconds later, Moddie announced his slipper tank was empty and his engine had cut. He got it started again, but, almost immediately, I heard the navigator telling Moddie that he did not have enough fuel to complete the flight to Israel. Mod-

die made a 180-degree turn and headed back toward
Rhodes in the direction from which we had come. I continued to keep my eye anxiously on the makeshift fuel gauge
on the right cockpit wall and worried about what was in
store for Moddie.

Not two minutes later my engine cut too. I turned
sharply over to the left into a dive and headed back while
restarting my engine. The Skymaster navigator confirmed
that I did not have enough fuel either. I told Moddie to
form on me and we headed back toward Rhodes.

After thirty minutes, worrying about the fate awaiting us,
we reached the island. I searched for an airfield and made
out two fields, Lindos in the south and a larger one near the
city of Rhodes. Not having been briefed on details of either
field, I chose the larger one and landed with Moddie behind
me. We taxied to the control tower.

IN A GREEK PRISON

A Greek Air Force officer approached me from the tower
and asked what we wanted. I said in my most innocent
manner, "We are short of fuel. Please ask the Shell agent to
come and refuel our aircraft. I have cash with me." Within
a few minutes he reappeared, not with the Shell agent but
with a squad of airmen armed with rifles. Thus ended the
second leg of our flight to Israel.

We were taken under guard to the Greek military headquarters in Rhodes and put in separate rooms with an
armed guard outside each door. The isolation soon began

to weigh heavily on me for I had nothing to read and there was no one to talk to. My requests to see Moddie were refused. The interrogation was headed by the base commander, Captain Vutsinas.

"Where did you come from? Why were you flying fighter aircraft with Israel Air Force markings and no cannons in the wings, and what do you want in Rhodes?"

I kept steadfastly to our story that we had set out from Israel on a long-range sea patrol and had run short of fuel. It is not difficult to understand the suspicions of the Greek commander and his intelligence officer, who was also present at the interrogations. Moddie was casually dressed in jeans, I was wearing a pair of brown corduroys with a sizeable tear in the seat, and I had a macho beard. I had a revolver in a holster around my waist and not one, but two bright, yellow life jackets. Worst of all was my South African passport with my real name and an Israeli identity card. It was in the name of Daniel Anan (*Anan* is a cloud in Hebrew) stamped with a communist Czechoslovakian visa. Profession: travel agent, which I chose at the time in a humorous vein. All this did not amuse the Greeks who began waking me at odd hours of the night for questioning.

The Greek Air Force officers had been scrupulously correct during their questioning. The men in dark suits who appeared at all hours of the night were members of the civilian counterintelligence and were of a different stamp. At that time in 1948, the Greek government was engaged in a bitter struggle with the Greek communist rebels led by General Markos. The rebel forces continually crossed over the border from Albania and Yugoslavia where they got their support. The Greeks told me they had found a map in my aircraft with a penciled-in course line running from Yugoslavia across Albania and the Greek Peloponnese, and on toward Rhodes.

The men in the black suits became more and more forceful, and when I kept to my story, they became exasperated and threatened to shoot me for being a communist. My protestations that I was not a communist—unlikely for someone from a wealthy background in Johannesburg—were to no avail. Realizing that the situation had become hopeless, the solitude and lack of communication with anyone began to affect me. Here I was, incarcerated in a prison in a strange country, not knowing the language, cut off from any contact with my people, and in fear of being shot.

After three nights of being woken up at all hours of the night for interrogation, I had a brainstorm. I remembered the friendship I had struck up with the Greek Air Force officer in the train overnight between Salisbury in Rhodesia and Johannesburg some five years before. Relying on the hope that George Lagodimus had survived the war in Europe, I told the Greeks about my meeting with George, whom I had invited to my home. I was not at all sure if he was alive or could be found, but I hoped he would remember our meeting in South Africa years ago. The Greek officers seemed puzzled but said nothing.

To my great surprise, a few hours later the door to my room was opened by the armed guard and in walked George Lagodimus wearing the uniform of a squadron leader in the Greek Air Force. As luck would have it, George had indeed survived the war and was still in the Greek Air

Force. They had sent an aircraft to Athens to bring him to Rhodes.

When George walked in I said, "Hullo, George, do you remember me?" Then came his shocking answer. "I am sorry but I don't know who you are." My scruffy appearance and the thick beard had misled him completely. I could not blame him, for our last meeting was on the other side of the world in South Africa years before I had even started flying and there had been no mention of Israel. After explanations on my part, reminders of our meeting and the visit to my home, George finally seemed to remember. He listened to my tale but, not believing our story of the patrol from Israel, told me to tell the truth and he left.

I did not see him again, and when I inquired about him a year or two later, I heard that he was among the officers who had supported King Constantine in his failed coup d'état, and he had been discharged from the air force. Captain Vutsinas was also involved, and I later heard he committed suicide after the failure of the coup.

During the interrogation, they kept on telling me that Moddie had broken down under questioning and had told the truth, and that we had indeed come from Yugoslavia. I became deeply upset when they told me he had been released and was back in Israel. I felt lost and angry with Moddie, whom I felt had betrayed me. Later, I found out that they had used the same trick on Moddie, but he knew they were not telling the truth. He had been placed in a cell between my cell and the kitchen, and, seeing that there was always another plate of food when his was brought to him, he had realized I was still there.

After five days of interrogation in Rhodes, I was flown in a Greek Air Force Dakota to Athens and was put in a cell in an air force police station in a suburb of the city. Again, Moddie was the lucky one. He again noted the two plates of food at mealtimes and guessed that I was still there, too.

During the questioning by the Greek Air Force, they asked me if I wished to see the South African consul in Athens. I refused their offer, for my activities were not on behalf of South Africa, and I did not wish to be an embarrassment to them.

Time weighed heavily on me in my solitary confinement. Besides the boredom, I knew that even without my Spitfire I was badly needed in Israel. I made chess figures from bits of paper and tried to play chess with myself. This lasted for a few hours, but I gave up after a short time. Except for washing, I was not allowed out of my cell and had no exercise. My mood deteriorated from day to day for I saw no possibility of my release.

The Greek army guards were stationed in the next room, and they played backgammon loudly all night long with little consideration for their prisoner next door. I shouted to them to keep quiet, but they paid no attention. Food consisted of Greek army rations, an unending flow of beans or some other vegetable covered in a meat sauce. The guards allowed me to go down occasionally into a freezing cellar where there were primitive cold-water washing facilities, and I rubbed myself down with my handkerchief.

After nearly two weeks, they told us we were both being released but would not be allowed to go to Israel because the United Nations had an embargo on the movement of men of military age to Israel. Moddie and I had an emotional reunion, hugging one another. We brought each other up-to-date on what had happened during the weeks of our solitary confinement.

Awaiting us outside the police station was a representative of Israel, George Georgiou, a Christian Greek born in Jerusalem. After throwing in his lot with the Jews, he had been appointed by Israel as liaison officer to the Greek government. Georgiou was a great help, and he and I became close friends. Years later in Israel, he turned to me for help in trying to save a failing industrial concern he had set up in Macedonia, and I was able to show my gratitude by arranging a bank guarantee for him. He now lives in England, and we are in contact to this day.

Contact was established with the Jewish community of Athens who showered us with gifts of clothing from one of the shops owned by Jews. Probably to celebrate our return to freedom, we both chose bright red pajamas and proceeded directly from the prison to the best hotel in Athens, the Grande Bretagne.

As we walked the streets of Athens, people pointed at us and seemed to know the whole story, probably from the press and radio. I must have been easy to identify with my beard and casual clothing. The Greek government seemed unable to figure out exactly who we were and why we were flying those unarmed Spitfires into Greek airspace.

The Greek Air Force confiscated our two Spitfires and later used them in their civil war against the forces of General Markos. One was lost in combat, and the remaining one was eventually returned to Israel—too late to be used in the war. Our release was on the condition that we abided by the UN regulation and did not depart for Israel. After some days a Pan African Air Charter aircraft arrived in Athens on its way to Israel. I went to the airport and persuaded the captain to take us. We boarded the aircraft and landed some three hours later in Haifa.

Unknown to me my mother had in the meantime arrived in Israel from Johannesburg, worried at not having heard from me for some time, and was overjoyed to see me. When she had first arrived in Tel Aviv and inquired as to my whereabouts, she was met by my friends and associates initially with a blank stare and then some cock-and-bull story of my being away in the Negev. Strangely enough, her flight, like all flights from South Africa to Israel at the time, passed through Athens and she had spent the night in the Grande Bretagne hotel a few days before I was released.

101 SQUADRON

After getting back to Israel, I was posted to 101 Squadron. I originally had been offered the command of Base Number Three, which was to be at Kfar Sirkin and the airfield from which our new Czech Spitfire squadron was to operate. During my time at Kunevice, I spent hours planning this undertaking, but when forward units of the Iraqi army advanced to within shelling range of Sirkin, the plan was scrapped. The Israel Air Force would make do with one fighter squadron equipped with its original complement of Messerschmitts, plus the Spitfires ferried from Czechoslovakia and three P-51 Mustangs now at our disposal. I was disappointed at losing my intended command of a second operational base but was quite happy to be a fighter pilot again and part of 101 Squadron.

Of the original six Spitfires that had departed Czechoslovakia on our first ferry flight, only three arrived safely. One crashed and two remained in Greece. When the three remaining fighters arrived in Israel, a crowd of bigwigs, including the prime minister, met the flight. As is known the Spitfire has no toilet facilities, and when one of them touched down after six hours' flying, the pilot pushed everyone aside and ran quickly to a corner to relieve himself before shaking hands with the dignitaries.

101 Fighter Squadron was based at Herzlia Airfield, a short rubble-covered strip at an angle to a longer one on the rich black loam of the agricultural land in the area. It was some fifteen kilometers north of Tel Aviv and next to Kfar Shmaryahu, a pleasant village of chicken farmers who hailed mostly from Germany. The pilots were billeted in the village in pastoral-like pensions, which usually catered for family holidays. The villagers were mostly former German professionals and not real farming yokels. One of the farmers turned his personal book collection into a lending library for us to use. Not surprisingly, our main fare consisted of chicken.

The peace and tranquility of the village and its European atmosphere made it highly attractive to us, and we spent many happy hours there. I was so taken with Kfar Shmaryahu that I vowed that if I ever settled in Israel I would make my home in the village. And I did. The occasional drunken parties we held were taken in their stride with equanimity by the staid farmers of the village. We soon felt at home, and one of our pilots bought a horse he named Gibor. I heard him raging bitterly at the paymaster when, as usually happened, pay was delayed for weeks, saying, "I have to feed Gibor. How for God's sake do you expect me to wait for my pay?"

We soon started flying operational missions. The squadron flew the Israel Air Force's first ground attack mission on 29 May 1948. An Egyptian armored column headed for Tel Aviv had gotten as far as Isdud, present-day Ashdod. After overcoming Kfar Darom and Kibbutz Yad Mordechai, the column, according to the boastful Egyptian radio commentator, would be in Tel Aviv within forty-eight hours. Indeed, when the Messerschmitts attacked, the Egyptians were a scant forty kilometers from the city. Our Czech-built fighters stopped the enemy's advance, but not without cost.

During that operation, we lost my close friend from the early days in the Air Service, South African Eddie Cohen, flying one of the Messerschmitts. After Eddie's death one of his friends, an American Mahal pilot from Atlantic City named Coleman Goldstein, asked me to arrange a scholarship at the Haifa Technion in Eddie's name. Unfortunately, the sum Coleman had, the entire savings of his Mahal salary from the day he came to Israel, was too small to do anything worthwhile, and we had to shelve the scheme. This intended donation by Coleman is one example of the camaraderie among the Mahal flyers.

Eddie was the first of the original nine pilots of the Sherut Avir to be killed in action. I knew he had crashed not far from Hatzor in the southern part of the Sharon plain, where we eventually moved with 101 Squadron from Herzlia. In November, during a lull in the fighting, I took off in a Piper Cub and found the crashed Messerschmitt not far from Hatzor.

I landed in a field near the crashed plane, but a deep wadi prevented me from getting near to it. I could not see any signs of a body, and as I had to keep the engine running, I took off immediately and reported my findings to Southern Command after landing. Hours later, the army telephoned to tell me that I was extremely fortunate for I had landed in the middle of a minefield. Eventually, the minefield was cleared and Eddie's body was found. He is buried next to the air force memorial in the Jerusalem hills. His mother came from Johannesburg to attend the funeral. I was deeply touched to hear her mumbling "Eddikins, Eddikins" while his body was lowered into the grave.

My only other contact with Southern Command was when two of us from the fighter squadron were invited to visit their headquarters in the village of Gederah a few kilometers from our field at Hatzor. The commander of the Southern Front at the time was General Yigael Alon, a well-known former Palmach commander. He had succeeded Yitzhak Sadeh. The atmosphere of the headquarters struck me as being very Palmach and kibbutzlike. In August 1948 Alon had become commander of the Southern Front. It was the most crucial front in the fighting at the time, because Egypt with its large standing army was the most dangerous of the enemies.

Alon's headquarters were located in a small house and

gave the impression of being businesslike and efficient with no trace of rank or special respect for the senior officers. While I was talking to Alon, the door to his room opened and in walked his deputy. I caught my breath, for here was the epitome of a Herrenfolk German officer. He was wearing a battledress without any insignia of rank like all of us, but the impression was unmistakable. He had a shock of blonde hair, steely blue eyes, and a ruddy, fair complexion with a turned-up nose. He was born a Sabra and his name was Yitzhak Rabin.

After the war Rabin was chief of operations at general headquarters while I had headed the air operations in the air force. We were in contact over a long period. Neither of us at that time could have foreseen that our families would in the space of a few years be linked and we should have a common grandson, Michael, after the marriage of his son to my daughter.

In time, Rabin became chief of staff of the Israel Army and commanded the forces that achieved the brilliant victory over the Arab armies in the Six-Day War of 1967. He eventually became prime minister of Israel. As the world knows, Prime Minister Rabin was assassinated by a right-wing, Israeli orthodox Jew in November 1995. Of course, Rabin's death was a great national loss as well as a personal loss for both me and my family.

Many of the Mahal volunteers who came from the West were Jews who had served in the Allied air forces, but there were also a few Gentiles. Most of them came because they identified with the Jewish cause. Three of our pilots were former Battle of Britain fighter pilots. Some were Canadians, some South African Air Force veterans, and others Americans with varying degrees of combat experience. There was no friction between the Mahalniks, and the Gentile pilots mixed happily with the Jews. In many cases these volunteers became very close to Israel.

The pilots of 101 Squadron were a wild lot. The staff of the Park Hotel on Hayarkon Street in Tel Aviv hastily removed chairs, glasses, and cushions as soon as they spotted a bunch of our pilots in their red baseball caps. Many of the hotel's furnishings were to be seen in our mess at the base. Apart from the drinking and the wild parties, we sometimes had to steal vehicles to get back to base. For many months Israel's sole fighter squadron's combat operations depended upon stolen cars. Such was the shortage of transport in Israel for months on end. One of the cars was a black Dodge belonging to the minister of health, but as a gesture of support of the government, we unanimously agreed to return it to its owner.

Among the Americans was a pilot by the name of Wayne Peake. He came from the Deep South, and his accent left his origins in no doubt. We called him "Hillbilly Boy." He shot down the "Shufti Kite" (In Arabic, *Shufti* means "look"). This was an RAF Mosquito XVI, which flew over Israel and our field at very high altitude day after day on photo-reconnaissance. For a long time, we were frustrated by the Mossie and often scrambled to intercept the fast airplane, without success.

On 20 November 1948, Wayne intercepted and shot the intruder down into the sea. On that occasion, he was scrambled in time, but the great height of the Mosquito was a problem because we did not have oxygen. Wayne became so disorientated by hypoxia—oxygen starvation—that he reported he had shot down a Halifax four-engine bomber.

When Wayne Peake died in the United States some thirty-five years after the War of Independence, he left instructions in his will that he be buried in Israel. A few of us former 101 Squadron pilots attended the service in the Christian section of the Israeli war cemetery near Haifa. Also the Canadian World War II ace Buzz Buerling and another Canadian Gentile volunteer are also buried in the same cemetery. Buerling had been one of the highest-scoring British aces and had particularly distinguished himself over Malta in 1942.

Another enemy aircraft that was shot down was a Transjordanian Rapide flying from Egypt to Amman. It crossed into our territory, and one of our pilots was scrambled and shot him down. According to our pilot, he warned the Rapide's pilot time and again by firing warning shots, which were ignored. We subsequently learned that one of the passengers was a well-known British press correspondent. The pilot should have chosen another route to his destination instead of over our lines in an enemy plane in the middle of the war.

Another Rapide, which trespassed over Israeli territory, came from Egypt after the end of the war, in June 1951, but on this occasion, the pilot heeded the instructions of the interceptor and landed in Beersheba. It turned out that it was one of the two Rapides I had bought in South Africa that had been confiscated by the Egyptians while flying to Israel in May 1948.

One incident gives some idea of the difficulties the Mahal volunteers faced, besides being far from their homes and their environment, not getting regular pay and fighting a war with comrades in arms with no common language. One 101 pilot was an American called Rubinfeld. He had served in the U.S. Army Air Forces and had a dark complexion. He did not know a word of Hebrew, and when his Messerschmitt was damaged by anti-aircraft fire, he baled out over the sea not far from Natanya. We believe he was shot down by Iraqi ground fire.

He landed near the coast and swam ashore. There was an Israeli army unit on the shore and almost no one had seen or heard of an Israeli fighter plane at that time early in the war. Because Rubinfeld was dark-skinned, they likely assumed he was an Egyptian. They covered him with rifles and cross-questioned him in a threatening manner. Rubinfeld knew no Hebrew, and the soldiers knew no English. The poor guy feared for his life and started shouting loudly "Gefillte fish, gefillte fish." This worked like a charm, and the soldiers helped him into dry clothes and brought him back to his squadron in Herzlia.

The Herzlia airstrip was in the middle of an orange orchard, and we camouflaged our aircraft among the trees. We covered them with striped netting so well that neither the British nor the Egyptian reconnaissance aircraft found us during the war. One day I flew a Piper Cub to the long dirt strip at Kibbutz Ma'abarot, which I had used to land the Spitfire. On the way back with my squadron-mate Giddy Lichtman, we saw a column of smoke from the direction of our Herzlia strip and three fighter aircraft circling it.

Thinking that the Egyptians had discovered our secret field and presuming that they had already bombed it, I dived low to try to escape detection by the enemy fighters. After a short while, we realized that the circling aircraft were from our own squadron. The source of the huge pall of smoke was from one of our Messerschmitts burning near the runway. When we landed I jumped out of my aircraft, yelling loudly to find out why no one was doing anything to get the pilot out. I was curtly told that exploding ammunition prevented anyone from getting close to the Messerschmitt. The pilot was my close comrade Moddie Alon, who had shortly before been in the Greek prison with me.

To this day no one is sure what happened. Moddie had returned from a mission in the south, had been able to get only one of his wheels down, and after circling the field twice, he had suddenly nose-dived into the ground. I think he was wounded and lost consciousness while trying to get the other wheel down.

At the time of his death he was the commander of 101 Squadron and had a great future ahead of him. His wife Mina, six months pregnant at the time, was nearby in the village, having come to spend some time with him the day before. A daughter was subsequently born and she bore his name and became our squadron mascot and a constant reminder of Moddie.

AIR BATTLES

The contrast between combat in the air and the everyday normality of our home in the pretty village when we returned often lent an unreal aspect to our days. Only in an air force does one encounter such contrasts during wartime. You wrap yourself in a flight suit, don a leather flying helmet, and after strapping on a parachute, take off, meet the enemy, and if you are lucky, return back home in less than an hour.

Toward the end of the war, our missions were only occasionally to strafe or bomb at low level as in the past. Most of our operations now became fighter missions, either escorting our bombers or patrolling in pairs looking for enemy aircraft.

As Israeli forces pushed the Egyptians back into Sinai, our sorties took longer. After we gained air superiority with our Spitfires from Czechoslovakia, we felt more secure from attacking fighters. We flew into the farthest reaches of the Sinai desert and penetrated enemy territory at the Suez Canal. We bypassed the main Egyptian air base of El Arish and continued over the forbidding wilderness of Sinai into Egyptian territory.

By October 1948 the squadron moved from Herzlia north of Tel Aviv to Hatzor, formerly a large RAF base closer to the main front of air activity in the south. Though most of our operations consisted of patrols and escorting C-46 "bombers" and B-17 Flying Fortresses, there were more dogfights in the last days of December 1948 and early January 1949. Our squadron's Spitfires, the remaining Messerschmitts, and two P-51s ran into Egyptian fighters on a number of occasions without losing an aircraft in the engagements. We shot down several Egyptian planes. I ran into Egyptian fighters a few times.

The first aerial engagement I had in the War of Independence was when I shot down a Dakota over El Arish. I spotted it as I was leading a flight of two P-51s supported by my squadron mate Rudy Augarten. I saw the aircraft far below in the circuit and couldn't resist the attack despite it being within the confines of the main enemy base. I shouted to Rudy, who grunted in return. Uneasy at venturing right into the lion's jaws, I feared they would shoot me down right over their field at such a low level. A moment's thought made me realize they could not open up on me with their anti-aircraft guns while I was in their circuit without endangering their own planes. I dived steeply toward the airfield.

Though I had my back to the Dakota from time to time, I struggled to keep him firmly in sight the whole time as I spiraled down from 10,000 feet to a few hundred feet. When I got down to his level, I approached at high speed from right behind him and made one long pass, firing from almost point-blank range while he was concentrating on landing. Rudy followed me down, firing, too.

The Dakota pilot aborted his approach and force-landed, wheels-up in the sand just outside the airfield. Though it was in the midst of the war, I did not feel very proud for it was a defenseless transport on its final approach. When I saw that he had crashed, I pulled up immediately after firing my guns and turned steeply to get out of range of the anti-aircraft guns at the airfield. I did not see a single anti-aircraft shell and realized that our attack was a complete surprise. I subsequently heard that the plane was piloted by a senior staff member of their headquarters, and though there were many wounded in the Dak, no one was killed.

Some years ago an American journalist who was writing a history of the air war was invited to the home of a retired wing commander in the Egyptian Air Force. While waiting for dinner and seeing a bullet displayed on the mantelpiece, he asked what it was. On being told that it was a bullet taken out of the Egyptian's chest when he was shot down during the Israeli War of Independence, he asked for exact details. When he heard the date, aircraft type, and time, he realized it was the Dakota I had shot down, for I had described the incident to him some time before in detail. I have tried—unsuccessfully so far—to locate the Egyptian so I can invite him to visit Israel.

I had two more aerial engagements with the Egyptians. In November 1948 my Mahal squadron mate Sid Cohen and I were patrolling near the Mediterranean coast keeping our eyes peeled at what was happening on the ground. But most of the time we concentrated on the sky in search of enemy aircraft. We weaved from side to side as we each covered the other's tail from attack. When I spotted two fighter aircraft silhouetted against the fawn-colored desert below and to the east of us, I prepared for the dogfight, increased engine RPMs, moved to rich mixture for more power at lower altitude, armed my guns, and turned steeply to get behind them. At the same time I shouted to Sid, who replied that he saw them too.

We turned to the east to come out of the sun. Owing to the proximity of the main Egyptian base of El Arish almost directly below us, we wasted no time in making a positive identification. After a quick look to ensure that we were in no danger of being jumped by fighters at a higher altitude, we dove to attack.

They looked like Fiat G-55s (later on we learned they were in fact Italian Macchi 205s), similar in appearance and performance to our Spitfires. They were flying too close a formation for aircraft on a combat mission so I presumed they were on a training flight.

Fortunately, we had the advantage of height and surprise. They did not see us until we got close to them, well above and behind. When I got close and had my adversary in my gun sight, I saw him start a turn to port, still oblivious of our presence. It turned into a classic dogfight with each of us trying to outturn his prey. I did not call to Sid again, but I caught a glimpse of him below me turning steeply as he got on the tail of his prey. It was clear no one at the large El Arish base below suspected us, thinking we were Egyptian fighters in the circuit.

As I prepared to fire, I was so surprised they were taking no evasive action I suspected that this was a trap and that they had protective cover above them. I hesitated for a few seconds to check behind me and, with my guns cocked and breathing heavily, saw them begin evasive action by increasing their rate of turn. I got on to the tail of my target and saw Sid doing the same below me. A number of steep turns with the sky and then the sea in turn filling the windscreen. My target panicked and went into a steep, wheeling dive to the southeast. That is the worst thing he could have done, for I was able to stay on his tail while retaining my advantage of height and speed.

He twisted and turned violently, and I followed his every maneuver. It was clear he badly lacked air-combat experience. The pilot of the lead aircraft seemed less agitated, but he, too, seemed not to know how to protect himself from the attack. I waited for them to change their direction in a turn from one side to the other to make it possible to catch them momentarily in level flight and to fire without needing a deflection angle. I pressed the firing button on my stick in two long bursts at very close range while I was right behind him as he changed direction in one panicky turn after another. Firing straight ahead, I could not miss. I saw the rounds from my guns hit his starboard wing with small pieces of the wing fly off.

When a big section of his wing disintegrated, he immediately went into a spin, slowly circling in an erratic path toward the ground far below. I saw no smoke or fire and quickly lost him in the murk below for I pulled up in a steep climbing turn to regain height as his craft hit the ground. There was no sign of a parachute. Being almost in the pattern of El Arish, I broke away sharply in a steep turn to starboard toward the sea. I saw no anti-aircraft fire.

I was subsequently credited with the kill and as I write this I can see the framed certificate on the wall above me. Sid received credit for the other Fiat as we reported them then.

THE LAST FIGHT

The day of 7 January 1949 was the last day of aerial battles in the Negev in the war and a memorable one for 101

Squadron. Our first patrol was to the southern Negev and Sinai in the early morning, with two of our Spitfires running into a flight of four unidentified fighters flying in our air space in the Negev. After a short battle, two of the enemy craft were shot down. After ours returned, a warning came through to the squadron that there were many fighters near our front lines, and we were ordered to send two aircraft out on patrol. We were puzzled that the warning given described the enemy fighters as "Bevin's Lemons," meaning RAF fighters. (Bevan was the foreign minister of Britain and was known to be a severe critic of Israel.)

I was on the second sweep, leading in a P-51, with Jack Doyle as my number two. Jack was a Mahal from Canada but retained his Irish brogue when excited or stressed. The Israeli troops, having routed the main body of Egyptian forces in the Negev, were in full cry as they advanced along the highway leading from the oasis of Abu Ageila just inside the Egyptian border toward Rafah near the coast. We patrolled above our armor, which was advancing along this important axis in the same area, where some days before I had removed the sole Egyptian Spitfire from among the dummy fighters on the El Arish satellite field.

Patrolling from Abu Ageila toward the Mediterranean, I spotted six fighters that looked like Spitfires flying far below us low on the deck above our advancing vehicles. I shouted to Jack but there was no acknowledgment. The road below was in use by our advancing forces, and the traffic was heavy. Some troop carriers, a few tanks, and artillery transporters were all moving as fast as possible toward the Egyptian forces fighting rearguard actions farther to the west.

Clearly, the flight of six fighters was not ours, and I had no doubt that they were Egyptian.

After scanning the sky above for some kind of escort, without waiting for an answer from Jack, I dived down out of the sun toward them, throttling back to the minimum to get down to the very low level of the enemy aircraft. With my advantage of height and the element of surprise, I headed for the enemy while trying to keep my speed up for an intended zoom upward after firing.

I got down well behind them, and when I realized that they had not seen me, I pushed the throttle forward and came at them from the same level, but at a much higher speed. They were low above our armor in line-astern formation: three pairs flying in a westerly direction toward Rafah. I was right behind and above them, and I selected the "Tail-End Charlie" on the left side for my burst of fire.

As I got down low, I saw him ahead of me in my gun sight. I shouted once to Jack but did not have time to see where he was, and I approached them out of the low sun in the east. As I completed my dive, I was right behind the enemy fighters at their level, but because of my dive at high speed, I had only split seconds for maneuvering. I closed in and fired one long burst. As I pulled up to the left in a steep climbing turn, I saw through my canopy dark brown smoke pouring from my victim. Surprisingly, he didn't appear to change his course. The rest of the flight seemed not to notice anything. They must have been concentrating on the action on the ground directly below.

As I pulled up I called Jack, asking, "Where are you?" There was an immediate answer in a very Irish brogue,

"Right with you, boy." I looked everywhere but Jack was nowhere to be seen. Now I felt that I was in trouble, for I was not willing to take on the five remaining Egyptians on my own. I lost sight of them in the early morning haze and returned to base in Hatzor.

After landing I went to the operations room and reported the engagement, claiming one probable because I did not see him actually crash into the ground. I reported the enemy as Spitfires because Freddie Fredkins, former group captain in the RAF directing us from the ground on the southern front, had reported them as "Bevin's Lemons," indicating that they were RAF. I met Freddie a short while after the engagement, and his description of the engagement compared closely with mine

From intelligence reports a long time afterward, we were told that the aircraft we ran into were, in fact, Egyptian Macchis. In the ops room after landing, I learned the six aircraft we surprised were Royal Air Force Spitfires. Whatever the final identity of the one I shot down, I hope it was not an RAF Spitfire, though they had no business being over our front lines at the time and therefore deserved what they got. I find it difficult to believe that the RAF was actively involved in the fighting on the side of the Arabs as some claim to this day. I know they helped with refueling, landing facilities, and supplies. I presume they passed on information from photo-reconnaissance missions as well.

The rest of 7 January was a busy day for 101. After the first two engagements, the next sweep consisted of two of ours, against eight enemy aircraft. One of our airplanes was flown by South African Arnie Ruch. Though there was an engagement, there was no claim of Egyptians shot down. There was a final sweep in the afternoon with our four Spitfires. The pilots who took part included Ezer and Bill Schroeder, the latter shooting down one of the British planes, which was later certified as a Tempest.

This great effort of putting up a flight of four fighters, never before equaled in a fighter patrol of ours, had brought our Spitfires up against twelve RAF fighters. Our pilots, with inferior equipment to that of the British (they had Spit XIXs whereas ours were old Mark IXs), knocked down another two, one of which was a Tempest making a total on 7 January of five RAF fighters shot down with no loss to us. Someone, I believe from 101, sent a telegram to the House of Commons in London, saying, "Sorry chaps, but you were on the wrong side of the fence this time!"

After these engagements with the RAF fighters, there was tension for a few weeks. The British aircraft were from the British Suez Canal bases and had a cozy relationship with the Egyptian Air Force. They had no right to have been where they were, and we were not happy about their incursions into the air space above our troops. On their side there was bitterness and loss of face for the way they had been trounced by what was for them an upstart air force. There were even fears that we were about to be embroiled in an Israeli-British war. However, the tension gradually passed and there were no more incursions by the Royal Air Force into Israeli territory. I believe that our success in shooting down four RAF Spitfires and one Tempest without any loss to ourselves must be attributed largely to the fact that we were battle-hardened fighter pilots with experience

from World War II and because we were flying tough combat flights daily, whereas the RAF pilots were from the Suez
Canal Zone with no recent operational time.

That evening, most of the pilots gathered at the Park
Hotel in Tel Aviv for a huge party. Everyone was drinking,
singing, and dancing until the early hours of the morning.
The South Africans entertained everyone with a Zulu war
dance, and all had a great time. It was a fine way for us to
relax and unwind from the tension of the final days of the
war. No one in the hotel this time minded the high spirits
of the 101 Squadron pilots in their red-peaked caps.

After all, scarcely eight months before, the Israel Air
Force had barely existed and had not possessed a single
fighter aircraft. Yet by 1 January 1949, Israeli fighter planes,
though outnumbered by as much as three to one, had
emerged victorious in the battles with the invading air
forces and had shot down the more-advanced fighters of the
RAF without any loss to themselves. This was an event we
deserved to celebrate and a fitting final victory for Israel in
its first war for survival.

Epilogue

AFTER the end of hostilities in early 1949 the foreign pilots who were my squadron comrades returned to their own countries. When they left I sometimes felt they were abandoning us in Israel. There was still so much to do. For me, acutely aware of our history throughout the ages, culminating in the Holocaust and the War of Independence, there was no choice. I felt I had to make my home in Israel to build up and strengthen this final haven for Jews at any time in the future. I have lived in Israel ever since.

Many of the volunteers who bore the brunt of the fighting in the air have from time to time reappeared for a squadron reunion or for a remembrance ceremony for pilots who fell in the war. We have kept in touch, despite the difficulties in sustaining the friendship cemented so firmly in 1948. Abroad in certain centers that supplied a large number of Mahalniks such as Los Angeles, Johannesburg, and London, ex-Mahal organizations have formed and meet occasionally. These meetings have served also to attend to the problems of families abroad after their loved ones were killed during the hostilities in Israel.

Others like me chose to remain in Israel and to make it our home. I have lived most of the time since the War of Independence of 1948 in the lovely village of Kfar Shmaryahu where 101 Squadron was born and from where its first battles were fought. Although I am the only former 101 Squadron pilot who lives here, there are Mahalniks of other units who have made their homes in this village. Other Mahalniks settled in various parts of Israel. All my five children are Sabras, born in Israel.

After the war I went to visit my family in South Africa. Within a few days, police officers appeared at our home and impounded my passport. No reason was given, but I cannot say that the South African government was at fault. Apart from my Irgun activities in England, two years before, my landing in Greece during Operation Velveta caused some diplomatic unpleasantness for South Africa. Moreover, South Africa was still part of the British Commonwealth at the time of the Israeli air battles with the Royal Air Force on 7 January 1949.

Without a passport there seemed no way for me to get back to Israel. But Universal Airways, the company I had formed a year before, agreed to take me on the next flight to Israel if I somehow got on the aircraft. Fortunately, they had a flight to Israel on Christmas Eve, and I boarded the plane at night during the festivities. After takeoff, the captain put me on the crew list to avoid problems on the way, and I returned to Israel. The impounding of my passport prevented me thereafter from again visiting the country of my birth for more than eight years. I was not allowed to enter the United Kingdom, either, for the same period.

After my return from South Africa, I was asked to set up a new air defense command because Prime Minister Ben Gurion was particularly concerned about the inadequate protection for the cities in case of enemy raids. The units were to include fighter-interceptors, anti-aircraft artillery, and a satisfactory early warning system based on radar. It meant starting more or less from scratch, and we set up a countrywide observer corps and a communications network. I relied to a great extent on what I knew of the air-defense system that operated in England during World War II and included also a unit of barrage balloons stationed near important targets. It was a major task, which I am proud to say we accomplished in record time, providing Israel with an adequate air-defense system.

Afterward, there was a period of some months during which we wrestled with the thorny problem of where to place this large group of units from various branches of the services. After obtaining information about how the problem was solved in other countries, and after paying a visit to the Swiss Air Defense Command, we incorporated the air defense command into the air force, which I rejoined as assistant chief of the air force. I retired from active service in 1952 with the rank of colonel.

A few months after completing this book, I was advised to contact the association of former crews of the outstanding PBY Catalina flying boat. I doubted I would make contact with the crew member who dived into the freezing Adriatic under heavy fire to rescue me so long ago. I wrote that though I was barely conscious at the time, his name remained indelibly in my memory for all these years. All I remembered was that he was an American and his name was Al Feliksa. I was dumbfounded when within a few days a reply came giving me his present address. I spoke to him on the telephone, and he told me he remembered the raid and my rescue. He was thrilled to hear from me.

Through the fog of my memory of forty-five years ago, I saw him as a tall, slim young man some two or three years older than me. The Catalina Association arranged for us to meet by a Catalina, and it was not surprising for me to discover he was a fine, caring American. I faced a quiet, much older American engineer, with no resemblance to the dashing young man who dived into the water. My emotions welled up, virtually preventing me from speaking. We discussed the rescue, which was carried out under heavy fire. I learned also that he was wounded during the operation. Now, Al uses his spare time to provide foodstuffs to destitute American families from surpluses in large chain stores. He had spent most of his life with General Motors and now lives in retirement in Michigan.

The reunion was hosted by the chief of the Canadian Air Force, and in my after-dinner speech, I made it clear that in my opinion Al and his fellow airmen are what is called in the Bible "the salt of the earth." As I told him, I have more than one reason to be an unabashed protagonist of the United States.

The meeting with Al after all these years has, together with the recording of the story of this book, brought my life full circle.

AFTERTHOUGHTS

The struggle for the rebirth of Israel and the "ingathering of the exiles" is unique in human history. I have tried to capture the spirit of the time and to give a picture of some of the events of that tumultuous period so important for the Jewish people and for Israel.

The War of Independence of 1948 was the climax of the struggle to return to their ancient homeland after 2,000 years of exile. Because of my involvement in that struggle, this tale is largely about the war in the air. It also focuses attention on the efforts of the Mahal overseas volunteers in achieving final victory. It was not only the deeds they achieved in that bitter war but also the living proof to the people of Israel that those in the Diaspora stand by them.

Furthermore, it may make it easier for our Muslim neighbors, our erstwhile enemies, to understand something of what has driven us to return to our ancient homeland.

The wars between Israel and the Arabs have been a bitter struggle between two just causes for one territory, and it is a matter of deep regret that fate and history have made us enemies on so many battlefields. Also, since the Six-Day War of 1967, a great number of Arabs have come under our rule in the conquered territories. I believe that we cannot for long continue to rule over people who oppose our reign. Not all Israelis are sufficiently aware that for the Arabs, their struggle is for a state of their own just as ours was. It is incumbent upon us to make peace at the price that must be paid, and to do it now while we are still strong, not in the future when Israel's strategic position may be less favorable than it is today.

After we have a final peace with all our Muslim neighbors, there will be no reason for us to fear the future, for if we look back into history, the Jews have throughout the ages invariably lived with less harassment in the Arab countries than in the West. There is no reason not to expect an enduring peace that will be to our mutual advantage. I believe that, despite the long exposure of Israelis to the culture and lifestyle of the West, we will get on well with our neighbors when peace is finally achieved.

We shall always have to face the dilemma of two claimants for one small piece of land. Without attempting to put into any equation of suffering the dispossessing of the former Arab residents of Israel with the horrors of the Holocaust for the Jews, however, it must be understood why we cannot seek to act only in accordance with hypothetical points of justice. Anyone who has any doubt about either the need, or the justice, of the struggle for a national home for Jews in Israel should be exposed to scenes of the Holocaust before passing judgment.

It is obligatory for all of us to remember how an advanced civilization went mad, believing that the mass murder of 6 million could provide the basis for the establishment of a New Order in the world. We must also recall how the world stood by and witnessed this greatest tragedy of human history without using every resource on earth to stop it.

With the passage of time, the maturing of Israel, and its final and complete acceptance by its neighbors, I believe that a shining future lies ahead for this old-new land, and there will be a fulfillment of the prophecy of Isaiah:

> For behold, I create new heavens and a new earth: and the former things shall not be remembered, nor come to mind. But be glad and rejoice forever that which I create: for, behold, I create Yerushalayim a rejoicing, and her people a joy. And the voice of weeping shall no more be heard in her, nor the voice of crying. Isaiah, chapter 65 verses 17 and 18

Index